Ye are the Light

Understanding the Kingdom of Heaven

Elena González

Copyright © 2020 Elena González. All rights reserved.
Published by Elena González
ISBN 978-1-67800-290-9

Dedication

I have heard it said that when the student is ready, the teacher will appear. I wish to express my heartfelt and eternal gratitude to my pastor and teacher, Dr. Harlo White.

For nearly 40 years, he has been an example to me of uncompromising courage in the face of overwhelming opposition. His unconditional love for the Body of Christ and his dedication to the ministry have been a source of inspiration to me and to the many sons of God whose lives have been blessed and transformed by his anointed preaching and teaching

May the Father continue to elevate him to higher realms of Glory.

Introduction

Why write a book about the kingdom of God? The fact is inescapable, even for a casual reader of the four Gospel accounts, that the ministry of Jesus was centered on the kingdom of God or the kingdom of Heaven. He preached about the kingdom, taught about it and He used parables to illustrate it to His followers.

To unlock the mysteries of the kingdom, we need an understanding of what the kingdom is, where it is and when it is. My hope and prayer is that this book, a compilation of articles written during a 20 year period, will answer those vital questions and that it will draw the reader into a closer fellowship with the King of Glory.

Just a few words about myself. I was born in New York City and thanks to the influence of a Godly mother and two Pentecostal aunts, I was exposed to the power of the Holy Spirit in my early childhood. During adolescence, however, I began a period of rebellion that was to last throughout my twenties. As my twenties drew to a close, I began to feel God drawing me to Himself. He began to reveal His unconditional love to me at the same time that He showed me my true condition and my need for a Savior. As Jesus became more real to me, bondages began to fall away. In December of 1981 I turned my life over to the Lord and I began to seek Him with a whole heart. The Father began to reveal things to my inner man concerning spiritual realities and warfare that I could not articulate.

I began to search for a church, a body of believers who were hungry for the Word and who desired to understand the deep things of God. I was searching for a manifestation of the anointing that would break the yokes that still remained in my life. In February of 1982, in Chicago, the Father led me to a powerful ministry and to the message of the kingdom of God. The heavens were opened to me...

In the years that followed, the Lord revealed truths to my spirit that I felt led to put in writing. The messages in this book came from an inner unveiling of revelation truths that were in agreement with the various outward teachings that the Holy Spirit has led me to over the years.

May this book bless and edify you. (All the scriptures cited are from the King James Version unless otherwise indicated.)

Contents

Truth or Ice Cream? 1
The Book of Hebrews 2
Are You Born Again or Just Saved? 10
I Thessalonians Chapter 4 14
The Last Day 18
My Kingdom is Not of This World 22
No Distance in God 25
Heirs of the Kingdom 28
The Hour Cometh and Now Is 31
Flesh and Blood 34
The Eye of the Needle 38
Christian Idolatry 41
Christian Vegetarianism 44
The Comings of the Lord 49
The Doctrine of the Physical Return of Jesus 53
Cast out the Bondwoman 57
Identity Theft 60
Fasting: The Dethroning of Food 64
The War Against the Second Birth 69
The Leaven of Herod 76
Laying the Axe to the Root 79
The Rent Veil 86

Enduring Faith..89
Emmanuel 92
Unless a Seed Die: The Mystery of the Third Heaven ...95
The Land of Milk and Honey... 101
The Spiritual Roots of Homosexuality 106
The Doctrine of Death.. 112
The Mystery of Our Union In God................................. 123

In the Beginning

Ye are the light of the world...

The Kingdom

It cometh not with observation, He said
Which interpreted means this:
His coming will not be televised.
CNN will not provide live coverage 24/7.
He will not be on the cover of Newsweek.
Christian, please don't bother booking your ticket
To Jerusalem to see him seated in a man-made temple.
His coming (unto them that look for Him)
Is an inside job.
Outwardly a quiet thing,
Inwardly a meltdown of your heavens and your earth,
As the Holy Thief robs you of all your treasure
Leaving you with only
His Presence.

Truth or Ice Cream?

Recently I came across a cartoon that the Spirit quickened to me. It was not hysterically funny, but it was loaded with spiritual insight. The scene was in heaven or what people conceive of as heaven (clouds). One man was standing under a sign pointing right that said "Truth" and the other man was standing under another sign pointed in the opposite direction that said "Ice Cream". The man under the Ice Cream sign said to the other man: "I'll catch up with you – honest."

The reality is that Truth comes at a price that not everyone is willing to pay. The Word advises us to buy of Him gold tried in the fire and to anoint our eyes with eye salve. The price tag for this divine nature and insight into the mysteries of God is very steep. It will cost you everything: loss of reputation, friends, family, untold hardships and death to everything that is not like Him. But the rewards surely outweigh the cost.

What do you say? Truth or ice cream?

The Book of Hebrews

In this study I wish to explore the book of Hebrews because it is such a treasure chest of the kingdom truths that have transformed my life. The Holy Spirit in this epistle is exhorting (Jewish) believers not to fall back into the realm of religious legalism and unbelief by reminding them who Christ is in us and who we are in Him. We are encouraged to press into maturity in Christ and to appropriate the fullness of the atonement.

Many Christians today have begun to receive a revelation of Christ "without sin unto salvation," a revelation that takes them beyond their initial understanding of Jesus as Savior carrying their sin and into a deeper revelation of who we are in Him. At this juncture in their spiritual walk, in the face of tribulation and the trying of their faith, many fall back - not into the world but into a religious spirit of unbelief - just as the Hebrews did in the early Church. The consequences are serious, then and now, when we fail to enter into the fullness of what God is revealing:

> For it is impossible for those who were once enlightened, and have tasted of the heavenly gift, and were made partakers of the Holy Ghost and have tasted the good word of God, and the powers of the world to come if they shall fall away, to renew them again unto repentance; seeing they crucify to themselves the Son of God afresh, and put him to an open shame. Heb 6:4-6

The kingdom truths in the book of Hebrews are so powerful and the Word is so plain that in this study I have merely organized scripture under themes that summarize the spiritual content. I pray that the Spirit of Truth will open up your understanding as you study these passages.

Heaven as a spiritual dimension not a physical place

> But ye **are come** unto mount Sion, and unto the city of the living God, the heavenly Jerusalem, and to an innumerable company of angels to the general assembly and Church of the firstborn, which are written in heaven, and to God the Judge of all, and to the spirits of just men made perfect and to Jesus the mediator of the new covenant, and to the blood of sprinkling, that speaketh better things than that of Abel. Heb 12:22-24

The unity of Jesus Christ and the believer

> For it became him, for whom are all things, and by whom are all things, in bringing many sons unto glory, to make the captain of their salvation perfect through sufferings for **both he that sanctifieth and**

they who are sanctified are all of one: for which cause he is not ashamed to call them brethren... Heb 2:10-11

Wherefore, holy brethren, **partakers of the heavenly calling**, consider the Apostle and High Priest of our profession, Christ Jesus...Heb 3:1

For we are made **partakers of Christ**, if we hold the beginning of our confidence stedfast unto the end...Heb 3:14

Death conquered by Jesus

But we see Jesus, who was made a little lower than the angels for the suffering of death, crowned with glory and honour; **that he by the grace of God should taste death for every man**. Heb 2:9

Forasmuch then as the children are partakers of flesh and blood, he also himself likewise took part of the same; **that through death he might destroy him that had the power of death**, that is, the devil; and deliver them who through fear of death were all their lifetime subject to bondage. Heb 2:14-15

The central place and power of faith

Take heed, brethren, lest there be in any of you an evil heart of unbelief, in departing from the living God. Heb 3:12

And to whom sware he that they should not enter into his rest, but to them that believed not? So we see that they could not enter in because of unbelief. Heb 3:18-19

For unto us was the gospel preached, as well as unto them: but the word preached did not profit them, not being mixed with faith in them that heard it. Heb 4:2

That ye be not slothful, but followers of them who through faith and patience inherit the promises. Heb 6:12

Now the just shall live by faith: but if any man draw back, my soul shall have no pleasure in him. Heb 10:38

Now faith is the substance of things hoped for, the evidence of things not seen. For by it the elders obtained a good report. Through faith we understand that the worlds were framed by the word of God, so that things which are seen were not made of things which do appear. Heb 11:1-3

The availability of the fullness of God in the Now

For we are made partakers of Christ, if we hold the beginning of our confidence stedfast unto the end; while it is said, **Today** if ye will hear his voice, harden not your hearts, as in the provocation. Heb 3:14-15

Having therefore, brethren, boldness to enter into the holiest by the blood of Jesus, by a new and living way, which he hath consecrated for us,

> through the veil, that is to say, his flesh; and having an high priest over the house of God; let us draw near with a true heart in full assurance of faith, having our hearts sprinkled from an evil conscience, and our bodies washed with pure water. Heb 10:19-22

> But **ye <u>are come</u> unto mount Sion, and unto the city of the living God, the heavenly Jerusalem**, and to an innumerable company of angels to the general assembly and Church of the firstborn, which are written in heaven, and to God the Judge of all, and to the spirits of just men made perfect and to Jesus the mediator of the new covenant, and to the blood of sprinkling, that speaketh better things than that of Abel. Heb 12:22-24

Deliverance from sin consciousness and the call to go on to perfection in Christ

> Who being the brightness of his glory, and the express image of his person, and upholding all things by the word of his power, when he had by himself purged our sins, sat down on the right hand of the Majesty on high...Heb 1:3

> If therefore perfection were by the Levitical priesthood, (for under it the people received the law,) what further need was there that another priest should rise after the order of Melchisedec, and not be called after the order of Aaron? Heb 7:11

For the law made nothing perfect, but the bringing in of a better hope did; by the which we draw nigh unto God. Heb 7:19

But into the second went the high priest alone once every year, not without blood, which he offered for himself, and for the errors of the people: the Holy Ghost this signifying, that the way into the holiest of all was not yet made manifest, while as the first tabernacle was yet standing: which was a figure for the time then present, in which were offered both gifts and sacrifices, that could not make him that did the service perfect, as pertaining to the conscience... It was therefore necessary that the patterns of things in the heavens should be purified with these; but the heavenly things themselves with better sacrifices than these. For Christ is not entered into the holy places made with hands, which are the figures of the true; but into heaven itself, now to appear in the presence of God for us: nor yet that he should offer himself often, as the high priest entereth into the holy place every year with blood of others; for then must he often have suffered since the foundation of the world: but now once in the end of the world hath he appeared to put away sin by the sacrifice of himself. Heb 9:7-9 & 23-26

Therefore leaving the principles of the doctrine of Christ, **let us go on unto perfection**...Heb 6:1

For the law having a shadow of good things to come, and not the very image of the things, can never with those sacrifices which they offered year

> by year continually make the comers thereunto perfect. For then would they not have ceased to be offered? Because that the worshippers once purged should have had no more conscience of sins. Heb 10:1-2

> **<u>For by one offering he hath perfected for ever them that are sanctified</u>**. Heb 10:14

The communion of saints

> And these all, having obtained a good report through faith, received not the promise: God having provided some better thing for us, that they without us should not be made perfect. **<u>Wherefore seeing we also are compassed about with so great a cloud of witnesses</u>**, let us lay aside every weight, and the sin which doth so easily beset us, and let us run with patience the race that is set before us...Heb 11:29-40 & 12:1

One final word, and this probably should be the subject of a study in itself, concerning the apparent contradictions in the Word of God. I say apparent because the author of the Word is the Holy Spirit and He does not contradict Himself. A battle goes on in the mind of the Christian who is not fully persuaded of the kingdom truths being revealed in this day. The enemy uses scripture to create confusion and double-mindedness. Only the Spirit of Truth can reveal the unity of the Word of God and teach us how to study to show ourselves approved and how to rightly divide the Word. The carnal intellect, trained in the doctrines of religion, must yield to the Holy Spirit if we truly desire to know Him and the power of His resurrection.

Are You Born Again or Just Saved?

There was a man of the Pharisees, named Nicodemus, a ruler of the Jews: The same came to Jesus by night, and said unto him, Rabbi, we know that thou art a teacher come from God: for no man can do these miracles that thou doest, except God be with him. Jesus answered and said unto him, Verily, verily, I say unto thee, Except a man be born again, he cannot see the kingdom of God. Nicodemus saith unto him, How can a man be born when he is old? can he enter the second time into his mother's womb, and be born? Jesus answered, Verily, verily, I say unto thee, Except a man be born of water and [of] the Spirit, he cannot enter into the kingdom of God. John 3:1-5

Many Christians totally misunderstand the words of Jesus in this passage. They assume that they are born again because they are partakers of the common salvation through faith in the atoning work of Jesus Christ. These Christians (Evangelicals, Charismatics and Pentecostals) hang their hopes on going to heaven when they die and they see the promise of that in this passage. In fact, for many, this "promise" is the chief motivating factor, along with the fear of eternal damnation, in going to the altar.

When Jesus said that unless you are born again you cannot see the kingdom of God, he was not saying, as most assume, that the reward for being born again is to one day see the kingdom of God. The key word is cannot (to be unable or incapable) as opposed to shall not. It was not a promise to be fulfilled in the future but a statement of a current reality. This is a crucial distinction. What he was saying was that seeing the kingdom of God is the proof that one is indeed born again. It is the very definition of being born again.

At best, what the great majority of Christians have experienced is the salvation of their spirits. One must be born again in order to go beyond the common salvation and to enter the kingdom of God where the mind, the emotions, the will and the body are transformed through submission to His dominion. To be born of God or born again is to begin seeing the way God sees, thinking the way He thinks. Without being born again, you will not be able to perceive the spiritual reality of the kingdom of God within you.

The kingdom of God or the kingdom of heaven (and both terms are used to describe the same reality) is not a location, a destination or something that is reserved for a future reign of Christ. It is all about His reign <u>in you</u> in the here and now. What confuses many are scriptures such as the following:

> Now this I say, brethren, that flesh and blood cannot inherit the kingdom of God; neither doth corruption inherit incorruption. I Cor 15:50

I want to deal first with the word inherit. The carnal mind is a sly and slippery thing. We all know that in the natural you inherit something when a loved one dies if he included you in his will. The death that triggers the inheritance is the death of the testator, not the death of the heir. Why is it then that when it comes to our spiritual inheritance our carnal mind is programmed to unthinkingly and automatically place the attainment of the inheritance in an afterlife? We look at this scripture, identify ourselves with "flesh and blood" and assume that we need to wait until we die to come into our inheritance.

But what is Paul referring to when he uses the term "flesh and blood" in the scripture above? To understand the term we need to go back to John. Among the New Testament writers, John had the fullest understanding of what it means to be born of God. (See 1 John especially 3:9 and 5:18 to give yourself something to ponder.)

> But as many as received him, to them gave he power to become the sons of God, [even] to them that believe on his name: Which were born, not of blood, nor of the will of the flesh, nor of the will of man, but of God. John 1:12-13

Those who "receive" him are born of God and their identity and life source are no longer in the Adamic flesh and blood. To receive is defined as: to take up with the hand or lay hold of any person or thing in order to use it, to take up a thing to be carried, to take upon oneself. When you are born of the Spirit you experience a change of identity, paternity and life source. You are truly a new creation. This goes far beyond merely believing that Jesus died 2000 years ago to pay the price for you to go to heaven after you die. Being a new creation goes beyond cleaning up your act by giving up all the things religion condemns. You cannot truly receive him now if you are waiting for him to appear in the sky. Do you see how the doctrines of man rob the people of God not only of their birthright, just as Jezebel robbed Naboth, but of their very identity as sons?

The system of religion tries everything in its power to prevent the conception of born again sons. It does this "spiritual contraception" by teaching lies and programming Christians to reject the spiritual Word, which is the supernatural seed of God that engenders sonship. (It is interesting to note how the religious system gets very judgmental and self-righteous about those things in the natural – contraception, abortion, fornication, adultery – that it is guilty of in the spirit. Which transgressions do you imagine are worse, the natural or the spiritual, in the eyes of God?)

In order to bring to pass His glorious plan of redeeming the creation from the bondage of death, God had to set aside for Himself a first fruits company of sons, the elect of God, in whom He is replicating His mind, His personality and the divine genetics that He created in the beginning. These are truly born again because they see with anointed eyes the unfolding of the kingdom of heaven within themselves. As God's dominion unfolds in our heavenlies, it will begin manifesting in our earthly dimension: our physical bodies. It is then that the creation will begin to see a body of people who are walking in the fullness of salvation: spirit, soul and body.

I Thessalonians Chapter 4

But I would not have you to be ignorant, brethren, concerning them which are asleep, that ye sorrow not, even as others which have no hope. For if we believe that Jesus died and rose again, even so them also which sleep in Jesus will God bring with him. For this we say unto you by the word of the Lord, that we which are alive and remain unto the coming of the Lord shall not prevent them which are asleep. For the Lord himself shall descend from heaven with a shout, with the voice of the archangel, and with the trump of God: and the dead in Christ shall rise first: then we which are alive and remain shall be caught up together with them in the clouds, to meet the Lord in the air: and so shall we ever be with the Lord. I Thess 4:13-17

The following statement caught my eye recently: "Redemption is the casting down of false images." We can never fully enter into what God has for us as long as we misunderstand His Word. I think this is especially true of this chapter. To understand God, we have to understand how He sees things and how He speaks. In the last verses of this chapter, God is describing not a future event that all Christians will experience at the same time, but rather a process that is even now occurring in the individual lives of God's people. This process can only begin when we begin to detach ourselves from our common, everyday understanding of words in order to enter into God's meaning.

This is not easy. Because, after all, a cloud is a cloud, a trumpet is a trumpet, the air is the air and an angel is an angel, right? Wrong! Especially when God is speaking prophetically as He is in these verses. These verses come alive with such richness and power when we see the spiritual meaning behind the physical symbols. What, then, is God truly saying when He uses the following symbols:

trump or trumpet – Paul refers to the trumpet as an instrument sounded to prepare troops for battle. It is far from being a signal to fly away over the horizon. In the book of Revelation, a trumpet represents a voice or message.

archangel – This represents a body of people who proclaim the message of God's kingdom. It is derived from the Greek word for messenger or pastor. The word evangelist is also derived from the same Greek root word.

dead in Christ – These are not Christians who have passed away. Those we think of as dead, God calls asleep in Christ. The dead in Christ are dead to sin and to the law. They have been crucified with Christ. They are not only dead, but also bound up in the grave clothes of religious traditions and bound by their carnal understanding of God's Word. These are the dry bones Ezekiel prophesied to which stood up and formed an army. What this passage is describing is the process whereby the dead in Christ are quickened ("the dead in Christ shall rise first...") by revelation truth. Once this happens, those who are now "alive in Christ" enter a realm of spiritual fellowship and communion with those who are now "asleep in Christ". This heavenly fellowship, which has nothing to do with an after-life, is what is described in Hebrews 12:22 & 23:

> But ye are come unto mount Sion, and unto the city of the living God, the heavenly Jerusalem, and to an innumerable company of angels, to the general assembly and Church of the first born, which are written in heaven, and to God the judge of all, and to the spirits of just men made perfect, and to Jesus the mediator of the new covenant...

air – The word that is translated as air in the King James Version is the Greek word meaning to breathe unconsciously. The word is a verb and not a noun and conveys the idea of a process that occurs in our spirits without our being fully conscious of it.

clouds – The clouds God is referring to here are not the vapor clouds containing particles of pollution, but rather Glory clouds containing ten thousands of saints. This same cloud of witnesses, as it is referred to in the book of Hebrews, covered Mt. Sinai when the law was given to Moses, it filled the tabernacle in the wilderness and also Solomon's temple in Jerusalem and it appeared to John, Peter and James on the Mountain of Transfiguration.

Just as the Glory cloud filled the temple in the Old Testament, God is in the process of revealing the fullness of His glory in His New Testament temple – our physical bodies. As this process unfolds, which is actually the coming of the Lord with the saints or in the clouds, we come into fellowship with those in the realm of glory just as Jesus fellowshipped with Moses and Elijah on the Mountain of Transfiguration.

The Christians in Thessalonica, like all too many Christians today, expected any day to see Jesus floating over the skyline of their city. They had conceived a false image. This is because God had not yet opened up their spiritual understanding and they were still seeing things through the eyes of Adam, the Old Man, or the man of sin or perdition as Paul refers to it in the second letter to the Church at Thessalonica. This "man of sin" is the natural mind of man that insists on seeing God and His Word in a physical and carnal way. The Word tells us that to be carnally minded is death but to be spiritually minded is life and peace.

The Father is sounding the trumpet today. His messengers are proclaiming the good news of the kingdom. He is equipping His army with the mind of Christ whereby we see things as God sees them. We are being caught up to a place in Him of such power and anointing that all the armies of hell will not be able to resist us. God's people are going to be raised up – not over city skyscrapers or mountain tops – but over the head of the enemy as we put all things, including death, hell and the grave, under our feet.

The Last Day

> No man can come to me, except the Father which hath sent me draw him: and I will raise him up at the last day. John 6:44

A message with the title "The Last Day" might conjure up images of dragons, beasts rising from the sea, scorpions, and a physical judgment seat – that is, until the Spirit of revelation begins stripping away from us the religious doctrines of man. In order to understand how God speaks in His Word, we must be delivered from the carnal imagery of the Adamic mind and the false concepts that are promoted and reinforced by man's religious teachings.

The Father is in the process of opening the spiritual understanding of His sons. God is unveiling the eternal plan of reconciliation and restoration and He is delivering His people from every aspect of our identification with Adam. When our spiritual understanding is opened, we have an insight into what God really means by the word "last".

The confusion arises because God does not use the word "last" in the sense that humans understand the concept. For example, if I have 3 dollars and I give 2 of them away, I will be down to my last dollar. It is an objective fact that I am down to my last dollar because my senses tell me that there are no more dollars left. That is the human understanding of the concept of "the last". So, the "last day" as understood by the religious mentality would be the day when we as humans can all agree with our senses that there are no more days. This concept is related to an outward event that happens to everybody at once and that we can all witness together.

The religious order of man, which God refers to as Babylon in the book of Revelation, uses this outward imagery and these human concepts to keep Christians on a spiritual treadmill. The fullness of God is never available in the "now" but always in a future day that will never be experienced, or in a life after death.

When God uses the term "last" it is not objective and outward but subjective and inward. To give you an example of what I mean, I would like to share an experience I had with the Father several years ago. At the time, I was working at a company that had a library. On my lunch breaks I would enjoy going to the library and reading, usually books relating to spiritual matters.

One day I was searching the stacks for a book I had read on a previous occasion. I was searching and searching when a thought entered my mind that I later realized was the voice of God. The thought said: "You will find the book in the last place you look." I laughed to myself and replied: "Of course I will find the book in the last place I look, because when I find the book, I will stop looking."

I continued with the search until it suddenly dawned on me that the Father had just given me a tremendous revelation of what He means by the last day or the last message. You are in the last day or the last message when you stop looking for another Day or another Message because you are fully persuaded that you possess the key to enter into all that God is. This persuasion, what Paul calls the most holy faith, must be ministered to us by the Spirit through the anointed preaching of the Word of the kingdom. Those who are still in the outer court or even in the holy place cannot lay claim to this persuasion. It is reserved for those who the Father is taking with Him into the bridal chamber or into the holiest of holies.

When you enter into this revelation, truly time is no more because the only function of time is to bring us to this very revelation. All that remains is for us to grow into this Truth. There is no other day or message to look for. "Today if you will hear his voice, harden not your heart..." (Ps 95:7-8). Once we have been completely absorbed by this revelation, both time and death are abolished in our own lives as we appropriate the atoning work of Jesus in its glorious entirety and as our total identification is with the Spirit Man, Christ, and not Adam, through whom death entered the creation. This is the raising up referred to in John 6:44 as our spirit and consciousness is raised to the heavenly realm.

For those sons who press into this place in God, the time is coming and now is when we can fulfill our divine appointments (kairos) as messengers of God. As we reside in the realms of eternity, we will intersect the human time line (chronos) with the revelation of light in order to bless and deliver those in captivity to darkness.

Then will the Word of God spoken by the prophet Isaiah come to pass in power and in truth:

> The spirit of the Lord God is upon me; because the Lord hath anointed me to preach good tidings unto the meek; he hath sent me to bind up the brokenhearted, to proclaim liberty to the captives, and the opening of the prison to them that are bound. Isa 61:1-2

My Kingdom is Not of This World

> Jesus answered, My kingdom is not of this world: if my kingdom were of this world, then would my servants fight, that I should not be delivered to the Jews: but now is my kingdom not from hence. John 18:36

All of the teachings of Jesus center on the kingdom of God. His ministry was to reveal that kingdom and, by his death and resurrection, to make a pathway for us to enter that kingdom. The scripture above, like so many passages of the bible relating to the kingdom, has been misunderstood by Christians to mean that the kingdom is available only in the afterlife. That interpretation, however, cannot be reconciled with the words of Jesus that the kingdom of God is within us. How can the kingdom be reserved for the afterlife if it is within us here and now?

The key to unlocking this mystery and seeming contradiction is in understanding what Jesus meant by "this world". The kingdom of God is not of this world yet is in us because we are not of this world. "This world" refers to the orderly arrangement of man according to the Greek word *kosmos* that is used for world in the scripture above. It refers to the systems of man, be they religious, political or financial.

Many of the followers of Jesus were disappointed in the nature of the kingdom he was describing and that he embodied. Like politicized Christians today, they wanted to impose the kingdom of God on unbelievers through political or military means. This is what the Emperor Constantine attempted to do in the fourth century after the early Church fell into apostasy. He tried to implement the kingdom of God by forced conversions.

Why did Jesus not want his disciples to use the means and methods of "this world" to implement his kingdom? We just have to look at the corruption of the Catholic Church beginning with Constantine and later with the so-called Holy Roman Empire when the world and the Church were plunged into the Dark Ages. In the effort to rule and reign in "this world" through carnal means, the gospel was darkened and the Word was made of no effect until the Reformation and the eventual separation of Church and State.

Another historical example of the fundamental misunderstanding of what the kingdom of God is can be seen in the rise to power of the Puritans in England in the seventeenth century. The Puritans used their military and parliamentary power to legislate puritan morality on an unruly populace. These efforts proved to be unsuccessful and counterproductive resulting in an inevitable backlash.

Why? Because Jesus intends for us to be agents of the kingdom of God planted in enemy territory, not to overtake it by military force or political power but to transform it, individual by individual, through the power of His Spirit and His love. Because it is "not by might nor by power, but by my spirit, saith the Lord of hosts" (Zech. 4:6).

No Distance in God

And John bare record, saying, I saw the Spirit descending from heaven like a dove, and it abode upon him. And I knew him not: but he that sent me to baptize with water, the same said unto me, Upon whom thou shalt see the Spirit descending, and remaining on him, the same is he which baptizeth with the Holy Ghost. John 1:32-33

One of the stumbling blocks for many Christians in understanding that the fullness of the Godhead is resident within us as spirit-filled believers is the fact that they spatialize, for lack of a better word, the Godhead. In the minds of most believers is an image of the Father and the Son out somewhere in what they call heaven with the Holy Ghost as the only representative of the Godhead here on earth.

    The problem comes down to a misunderstanding of what actually transpired on the day of Pentecost as those patient and dedicated 120 people waited in obedience to the direction of the resurrected Jesus. Let us look at another scripture, again from John's gospel, to see the source of the problem:

> Nevertheless I tell you of a truth: It is expedient for you that I go away: for if I go not away, the Comforter will not come unto you: but if I depart, I will send him unto you. John 16:7

From this scripture, specifically the word "send," Christians have formed the mental image of Jesus delivering the Holy Ghost to the Church from a distance as we would send a package via FedEx. If this had been the case and the Holy Ghost is a separate entity, how was the prophetic word in John 1:32-33 cited at the beginning of this chapter fulfilled? In a passage of scripture that totally negates the rapture doctrine and the teaching that there will one day be a physical "second coming" of Jesus, he tells the disciples about the upcoming day of Pentecost:

> I will not leave you comfortless: I will come to you. Yet a little while, and **the world seeth me no more**: but ye see me: because I live, ye shall live also. At that day, ye shall know that I am in my Father, and ye in me and I in you. John 14:18-20

The fact of the matter is that the three aspects of the Godhead are inseparable though distinct in function. This becomes clearer when we take a closer look at the Greek word *pempo* that was translated in the scripture above (John 16:7) as "send." *Pempo* means to dispatch from the subjective point of departure, to transmit, bestow or wield. It is the exact same word that in Revelation 14:18 is translated **thrust in** (Thrust in thy sharp sickle....). What actually happened on the day of Pentecost was that Jesus in spirit form transmitted, bestowed, wielded and *thrust himself into* those 120 saints thereby making their bodies His body for the continuance of His ministry.

The Holy Ghost is not some kind of third rate manifestation of the Godhead sent from afar to hold our hands while we wait for the return of the real thing. The Church has for too long maligned the Holy Ghost by not appreciating the fact that He is the means by which we are joined in holy union to the Son who contains within Him the fullness of the Godhead bodily. And the body referred to by Paul in Colossians 2:9 is no longer the physical body of Jesus, which served its purpose and the world will see no more, but <u>our</u> physical body.

Heirs of the Kingdom

> Now this I say, brethren, that flesh and blood cannot inherit the kingdom of God; neither doth corruption inherit incorruption. I Cor 15:50

The scripture above is so often misunderstood by Christians that it bears closer examination with an open mind and a receptive spirit. The first misconception is the notion, held by many Christians, that our inheritance in Christ Jesus will be claimed in the afterlife. It is very important to understand that in the Spirit, just as in the natural, it is the testator's death that enables his heirs to inherit, not the heir's death. In fact, if an heir dies without finding out about his inheritance, he simply loses what could have been enjoyed in this life.

Sadly, such is the fate of millions of Christians who go to the grave in ignorance of what was rightfully theirs through the death and resurrection of Jesus. As the scripture says, truly His people perish for the lack of knowledge.

Many Christians that do understand that the kingdom of God is for this life often cling to dispensational doctrines that declare that the kingdom is for another time (when Jesus comes back to rescue us), another place (Old Jerusalem), or for another people (natural Israel). However, the inconvenient truth that does not fit into dispensational doctrine is that the kingdom of God is within us. The "flesh and blood" mentioned in this scripture refers to our Adamic nature and natural genetics, not our physical bodies. Nobody inherits the kingdom simply by being a natural Jew or a natural anything else.

In the context of this scripture, Paul is drawing the distinction between the natural man, Jew or Gentile, and the spiritual man who by virtue of being born again has the seed of God growing within him. The kingdom is within him and he is a citizen of God's kingdom without having to wait for any future event. King Jesus, who scripture declares seated Himself on the throne of David at His resurrection (see Acts 2:30-31), has made His habitation in us. He does not need to seat Himself on any man-made throne in a man-made temple constructed at some future point in time. If we allow His life to take us over, we will rule and reign with Him right now.

The Old Testament experience of the children of Israel as they entered the Promised Land provides a metaphor for us in understanding our inheritance and how to take possession of it. (It is instructive that for the generation of Jews that left Egypt the punishment for disobedience was death. Physical death was not portrayed by God as the entrance into a reward but rather as a mark of falling short of the promise.) Canaan in the Old Testament was a mere figure of our true inheritance. It amazes me that Christians identify the kingdom of God with a sliver of desert land in the Middle East.

When God commanded the children of Israel to fully possess the land by destroying the occupants, He was pointing to an inheritance that cannot be measured in square miles or geographical boundaries. He was pointing to our dominion over all the earth. This dominion will be accomplished as we learn to rule and reign over every aspect of our own being – spirit, soul, mind and body – in His Name.

In a very real sense, we are the Promised Land and our physical body is the earth that is inherited by the meek or those who manifest His Nature. Just as the children of Israel had to go into every corner of the Promised Land to dispossess the ungodly inhabitants, we need to walk this inheritance out by subduing every enemy of God within us. The last enemy of the kingdom to be conquered is the death that is working in our physical bodies.

Rest assured that there will be a people who will experience this and will reach this mark of the high calling that Paul strove for. In order to reach that goal, God's people need to develop an overcoming faith and they need to be delivered from the doctrines of devils that have put His promises just out of reach when in reality they are available here and now to those who have the faith to attain them and the burning desire to walk in the fullness of our inheritance.

The Hour Cometh and Now Is

> But the hour cometh, **and now is**, when the true worshippers shall worship the Father in spirit and in truth: for the Father seeketh such to worship him. John 4:23

> Verily, verily, I say unto you, The hour is coming, **and now is**, when the dead shall hear the voice of the Son of God: and they that hear shall live. John 5:25

What Jesus was pointing to in these scriptures is something that runs totally counter to current religious teaching and especially the branch of religious thought called "eschatology" or "end times" theology. This theology focuses on a future outward event that will be glorious for believers and catastrophic for the ungodly. What Jesus was saying is this: when you really begin to hear My voice, in that hour, in that very moment, you will be ushered into a new place in Me of resurrected Life and spiritual intimacy.

This is a necessary and crucial transition and the beginning of a process of spiritual transformation as we grow in that most holy faith that few Christians know anything about. If the faith that pleases God comes from hearing, how can you please God if you cannot hear His voice?

I am talking about a place where you finally grasp that God is a Spirit and that His Word is spiritual and that it must be fulfilled first in your spirit man. As the Samaritan woman began to understand after her spiritual ears came open, "holy" cities or "holy" mountains are irrelevant. The holy place is in our spirit and nowhere else.

In the hour that you truly receive that insight, you have risen from the realm of death and the grave of your carnal understanding and have entered into the realm of the resurrection Life contained in Him. In that very hour is fulfilled the prophecy in the book of Revelation that speaks of the fall of Babylon (the type or symbol of dead religion). In that hour, for you, Babylon has been judged and has fallen. We can see here the crux of biblical prophecy. When you get right down to it, all prophecy needs to be fulfilled in us or it does us no good. The children of Israel had to come out of Egypt but until Egypt came out of them, they were still slaves to it.

What good would it do me if the world system, including the religious system, collapsed if I remain in bondage to those systems? Moreover, what good would it do me to see Jesus in the sky or to be raptured away from the earth if I have not overcome in every area of my life?

Many Christians take great comfort in the scripture that says that when we see Him we will be like Him. For those who are anticipating a magical event that does not require anything on their part, the only thing that awaits them is God's fiery purification in the next realm if they try to avoid it in this realm. No, that scripture does not refer to a magical event but rather to a process that begins with hearing Him and culminates with His Life totally taking us over so that we see Him in ourselves.

Until you have heard His voice, until your spirit has been quickened by this revelation, you are under the bewitching spell of a religious system that wants to point you to an outward future event and your soul will be utterly complicit with this deception. The spell is broken in the hour that you finally hear His voice and begin to see His Word in a new light.

Until then, throughout every generation, He will patiently ask the question: Can you hear Me now?

Flesh and Blood

> Now this I say, brethren, that flesh and blood cannot inherit the kingdom of God; neither doth corruption inherit incorruption. I Cor. 15:50

> And Jesus answered and said unto him, Blessed art thou, Simon Barjona: for flesh and blood hath not revealed it unto thee, but my Father which is in heaven. Matt. 16:17

These two scriptures, considered together, illustrate an important aspect of the kingdom of God that is not understood by many Christians today. They look at the first scripture and conclude, wrongly, that the kingdom of God is reserved for the afterlife. Or, again wrongly, they make a distinction between the kingdom of God and the kingdom of heaven by arguing that the first is for our lives here and now and the second is for the afterlife.

The fact, however, is that these two terms are used interchangeably in scripture. In Mark 1:15 Jesus exhorts us to repent and believe the gospel or good news because the kingdom of God is at hand. In Matthew 3:2 the term kingdom of heaven is used by John the Baptist to describe what is at hand. See also Luke 7:28 and Matthew 11:11 where the identical words are spoken by Jesus, once using "heaven" and once using "God". In Matthew 19:23-24, Jesus uses the terms interchangeably.

The second scripture quoted above shows that this "flesh and blood" cannot be synonymous with our physical bodies, although there is a definite relationship there that needs to be understood. This "flesh and blood", whatever it is, can be overridden and overcome while in the physical body by the power of God. In this exchange between Jesus and Peter we see laid out before us a parable of how we enter the kingdom of God where flesh, or our carnal understanding, counts for nothing and blood, or our genetic background, counts for nothing. The truth of who Jesus Christ is becomes foundational to enter the kingdom of God and, as we see here, God had to override Peter's fleshly intellect to impart that revelation.

Just as our carnal intellect or our theological training cannot understand, apprehend or enter into the kingdom of God, our genetics (or blood) does not count for anything with God. Inheritance of the kingdom is by divine revelation and faith, not by bloodline. There is neither Jew nor gentile...

When we are born again and positioned in Christ we take on His name, His identity, His flesh and His blood even as we walk around in these "flesh and blood" physical bodies. We become heirs who have entered into our inheritance: the land of milk and honey, the kingdom of God.

Higher Ground

Take heed therefore that the light which is in thee
be not darkness...

To Laodicea

The enemy is not Darwin,
Nor evolution, nor dinosaur bones.
The enemy is not liberals, democrats, the NY Times,
Feminists, homosexuals or jihadi terrorists.
The outside world – for whom Christ died – is not the enemy.
No, the enemy of the Cross is the world inside God's people:
> *ignorance where there should be understanding*
> *superficiality where there should be depth*
> *pride where there should be humility*
> *blindness where there should be vision*
> *letter where there should be Spirit*
> *doctrine where there should be revelation*
> *hatred where there should be love*
> *darkness where there should be light*
> *division where there should be unity.*

Truly, God's enemies are those of His own household.

The Eye of the Needle

Jesus said unto him, If thou wilt be perfect, go and sell that thou hast, and give to the poor, and thou shalt have treasure in heaven: and come and follow me. But when the young man heard that saying, he went away sorrowful: for he had great possessions. Then said Jesus unto his disciples, Verily I say unto you, That a rich man shall hardly enter into the kingdom of heaven. And again I say unto you, It is easier for a camel to go through the eye of a needle, than for a rich man to enter into the kingdom of God. When his disciples heard it, they were exceedingly amazed, saying, Who then can be saved? But Jesus beheld them, and said unto them, With men this is impossible; but with God all things are possible. Matt 19:21-26

At a recent family gathering, the Lord quickened this passage of scripture to me regarding the rich man and the eye of the needle. As I listened to the conversations around me, I was wondering why it is that the unsaved members of my family were so resistant to the Gospel. The Lord spoke into my spirit that it is their riches that keep them out of the kingdom. He was not referring to material wealth in regard to my family and, I believe, if we examine the scripture above carefully, we have to conclude that He wasn't necessarily referring to material riches in Matthew 19.

The key is in the response of the disciples who "were exceedingly amazed, saying, Who then can be saved?" The disciples knew that Jesus was making a very radical statement that went beyond the popular truism that material wealth corrupts and that rich people, as we commonly think of them, are attached to their money. As spiritually obtuse as His disciples oftentimes were, in this instance they had a revelation of the fullness of what Jesus was pointing to as the obstacle to attaining Life (zoe) and the kingdom. Had they understood Jesus to be referring to material wealth, their response would have been more along the line of: "Whew! It's a good thing most folks, like us, are not rich!"

The fact of the matter is that Jesus had some rich followers who were not required to give all their possessions away. Although the rich young ruler in the teaching had evidently made an idol of his material wealth, the disciples understood that Jesus was getting at something more universal and insidious: anything we value more than our relationship with Him or anything that keeps us from moving higher in Him constitutes our riches. The deepest strongholds are actually not material, but in the mind: intellectual pride, political ideologies, world views, theologies, philosophies, paradigms, religious doctrines of men. These are the riches that keep the unsaved and many Christians from entering into the kingdom.

The eye of the needle is like the birth canal from which we emerge stripped of all our riches in the process of being born again – the prerequisite for even seeing the kingdom. As for entering the kingdom, we need to have an open heart and unfettered mind like the little child who has no intellectual or doctrinal baggage.

An interesting twist to all this is that the scripture quoted above, along with some other sayings of Jesus regarding "the poor" and some verses in James, have been the foundation for the Catholic theology of poverty which glorifies poverty as a means to a closer relationship to God. (The exceptions, of course, were the popes and bishops, who supposedly had the obligation of manifesting and surrounding themselves with the wealth of the "kingdom").

Unfortunately, the Holiness/Pentecostal movement adopted the theology of poverty by teaching that poverty was God's way of keeping us humble and protecting us from worldliness. In the Pentecostal theology of poverty, everything connected with prosperity becomes suspect.

This development is an ironic twist and a clever ploy of the enemy because the very theologies of poverty – based as they are on a limited and superficial understanding of the teachings of Jesus – become an example of the "riches" that keep Christians from entering into the kingdom or even understanding what or where the kingdom is.

Instead of ministering an entrance into the kingdom of God, these theologies, for Protestants and Catholics alike, keep our focus on outward things. Ultimately, they block entrance into the kingdom of God by becoming an obstacle to understanding the fullness of the mind of Christ.

Christian Idolatry

The other day I received a forwarded chain email that I found very disturbing, but not for the reason the original sender intended. Even more disturbing was the fact that it came from a son of God who should know better. Let me describe it as best I can recall and see if you can understand what I found offensive.

The email was basically a series of photographs of US soldiers either in action, at rest or wounded. It ended with these words: There are only 2 people who have died for you:

1. Jesus Christ
2. The US soldier.

This was followed by an encouragement to support the troops. That was it.

From the title of this chapter and for those who are familiar with my writings, by now you may have guessed where I am going with this. Let me first make it very clear that my heart really goes out to those brave men and women who serve in the US military. I have often been moved to tears at the sight of one of their coffins and at the thought of their young lives being cut short. I truly love this country and the principles for which it stands.

But I see this email as a symptom of a deep malaise in the Body of Christ in this country which I want to briefly address.

Partly because we live in a so-called Christian society, many of God's people have been seduced by a watered down Christianity that is more cultural and political than spiritual. We have used Jesus and Christianity to serve a "larger" purpose: the pursuit of political power and cultural influence. We have replaced God's purposes with our own earthly agenda.

We have not understood that there is no purpose greater than the purpose of God: to raise up a perfected Church that knows no geographical boundaries and flies under no national banner. Viewed in this light, we can see that patriotism has become an idol lodged in the hearts of many of God's people in this country. It is this idolatry that makes it perfectly reasonable to refer to the sacrificial work of Jesus in the same breathe that we talk about the US soldier. There wasn't even a double-space between the lines!

The account of the passage of the children of Israel into the Promised Land provides a dramatic illustration of what I am trying to say here:

> And they commanded the people, saying, When ye see the ark of the covenant of the LORD your God, and the priests the Levites bearing it, then ye shall remove from your place, and go after it. Yet there shall be a space between you and it, about two thousand cubits by measure: come not near

unto it, that ye may know the way by which ye must go: for ye have not passed this way heretofore. Joshua 3:3-4

This long distance between the ark (a type or symbol of Jesus) and the rest of the children of Israel as the ark was carried by the priests into the river Jordan symbolizes something profound about the atoning work of Jesus and what He accomplished for us in conquering hell, death and the grave. Nothing can touch it. Nothing comes near it. Anything that diminishes that atoning work is an idol.

As Christians we need to jealously guard those two thousand cubits.

(My eternal thanks for the life and writings of T Austin-Sparks.)

Christian Vegetarianism

> Whom shall he teach knowledge? and whom shall he make to understand doctrine? them that are weaned from the milk, and drawn from the breasts. Isa 28:9

> Surely I have behaved and quieted myself, as a child that is weaned of his mother: my soul is even as a weaned child. Psa 131:2

As you may have guessed, this is not a chapter about natural food or the eating habits of some Christians. Much can be said on that topic, but that would be the subject for another discussion.

In the first passage quoted above, the Lord seems to be saying that the key to divine knowledge and understanding is to leave the milk behind. When God exhorts us in the Old Testament and the New to move from the milk of His Word to the meat, what is He referring to? What is the connection between the soul and the milk? What constitutes milk and meat and why will we never truly know or understand Him if we remain on the milk? Why is it so important to Him that we make that progression?

Our loving Father provides the answers to these questions, for those who have ears to hear and a heart to receive, in the powerful fourth chapter of Paul's letter to the Galatians.

To give a brief background to this letter, Paul addresses Gentile believers in Galatia in some of the strongest language in the New Testament because they were being seduced by Jewish Christians. This seduction or bewitching, as Paul refers to it, was the effort on the part of the Jewish Christians to bring the Gentiles under the Jewish law with the insistence that they be circumcised and that they observe Jewish ordinances and feast days. Paul was gravely concerned that this judaizing of Gentile Christians was undermining the gospel of grace and inclusion. The Galatians would start to view themselves as somehow inferior to the Jews as the Church in Galatia was threatening to become a Jewish wannabe body. I imagine that Seders, prayer shawls and shofars were becoming all the rage among Galatian Gentiles. Sound familiar? Let's look at verses 21-26:

> Tell me, ye that desire to be under the law, do ye not hear the law? For it is written, that Abraham had two sons, the one by a bondmaid, the other by a freewoman. But he who was of the bondwoman was born after the flesh; but he of the freewoman was by promise. Which things <u>are an allegory</u>: for these are the two covenants; the one from the mount Sinai, which gendereth to bondage, which is Agar.

For this Agar is mount Sinai in Arabia, and answereth to Jerusalem which now is, and is in bondage with her children. But Jerusalem which is above is free, which is the mother of us all.

These verses are a Holy Spirit tutorial on how to understand the Old Testament. In one brilliant paragraph, Paul demolished all the concepts that derive from a literalistic, carnal reading of the Word (the milk) and elevates and illuminates the Word in its true meaning which is contained in types (symbols) and shadows of Christ and His Church (the meat). Paul is seeking here to forge a spiritual identity for these Gentile converts by highlighting their union in the Spirit with Old Testament believers. We are one bread in Christ Jesus (I Cor. 10:17) with the faithful in the Old Testament. He imparts to those Galatian Gentile Christians (and all of us) the very real sense that they are on an equal footing with Jewish Christians as children of the Jerusalem that is above. In fact, as far as carnality is concerned, Jews that reject Jesus Christ as their messiah are no different in the eyes of God than the natural descendants of Hagar (the Arabs). They are all children of the Jerusalem which now is (natural Jerusalem) with its legal bondage to the Koran or the Torah.

If Christians of all stripes and denominations would prayerfully meditate on these verses with an open mind and what they tell us about how the Old Testament is to be understood, all sorts of doctrinal bondage would fall away. For Catholics, the fact that it is Sarah and not Mary who is the type (symbol) of the mother of us all, heavenly Jerusalem, should cause them to re-evaluate their church's teachings. For Evangelicals, Pentecostals and Charismatics, these verses are the key that unlocks the meaning of Old Testament prophesy in regard to "Israel". Who is God's true Israel? The milk might lead you to believe it is natural Jewry, but the meat reveals the truth.

The sad truth, however, is that so many Christians are deeply brain-washed and just plain lazy or fearful. As the second scripture quoted at the beginning of this chapter shows, there is a connection between the milk and the soul realm. Our soulish emotions often keep us from moving into the meat of God's Word. Why? Milk does not cause waves and guarantees acceptance by the religious establishment whereas meat often brings persecution. Milk goes down easy but meat requires work. Just as in the natural we need teeth to take apart the fibers of meat and we need to make the effort to chew and digest that meat, we need to take the Word of God apart, study it, go to the original languages, and prayerfully meditate on the true meaning. We need to be <u>hungry</u> for more of God, not complacent, and willing to die to everything Adamic that keeps us from totally pleasing God.

Why is this so important to God? Because our God is a Spirit and His Word is spiritual. He wants to raise up a nation of people who are like Him and like His Word. The woman at the well in Samaria discovered this. This woman is a type or symbol of many Christian Churches today that are married to the five senses and in bondage to man. (This is the meat revelation. The milk interpretation portrays her as a loose and immoral woman with a shady marital past. Which interpretation provides an insight into the mind and heart of God?) The Samaritan woman wants to know whether she should book her flight to Jerusalem for the second coming.

Her theology, like the theology of many Christians today, was a carnal mess but Jesus straightened her out by quickening her spirit man. If you want to worship God, He told her, if you want to please Him, you must worship Him in Spirit and in Truth.

The milk will never bring you to the knowledge and understanding of His eternal plan, but the meat will. Beloved, seek Him in the deep things of His Word!

The Comings of the Lord

O Jerusalem, Jerusalem, which killest the prophets, and stonest them that are sent unto thee; how often would I have gathered thy children together, as a hen doth gather her brood under her wings, and ye would not! Behold, your house is left unto you desolate: and verily I say unto you, Ye shall not see me, until the time come when ye shall say, Blessed is he that cometh in the name of the Lord. Luke 13:34-35

I recently read an article that cited the above scripture as evidence that all natural Israel will be saved through the physical return of Jesus to the city of Jerusalem. To the contrary, I believe that this scripture (for those who have ears to hear) is saying something very different to natural Israel regarding the manner of His coming (or His comings...but I will get to that later).

For the nation of Israel, the ministry of Jesus represented the last chance for the Jewish nation, en masse, to turn from their rebellion and unbelief and accept Him as Messiah. He came to His own to fulfill and complete the Law and to usher in the age of the Spirit which was dynamically inaugurated on the day of Pentecost. On that glorious day, the Spirit of God began the fulfillment of the prophecy of Jesus in Luke 22:29-30:

> And I appoint unto you a kingdom, as my Father hath appointed unto me; That ye may eat and drink at my table in my kingdom, and sit on thrones judging the twelve tribes of Israel.

Those Jews from every corner of the world who gathered at Jerusalem on that day of Pentecost represented the 12 tribes of Israel. As the 120 disciples poured out of the upper room anointed with the Spirit of the risen Christ, the Jews who gathered around them were in actuality standing before the judgment seat of God. On that day, 3000 Jews responded to the call to repentance and every day since then, individual Jews have responded to that same call.

I believe that in the coming years multitudes of Jews (as well as Moslems, Buddhists, Hindus, etc.) will receive Jesus as Messiah and Savior. But it will not be as a result of Jesus returning in a physical body to inhabit a physical temple in a physical city in the Middle East.

We need to understand verse 35 in Luke 13 (quoted above) to see how these massive conversions will take place. The interpretation of this scripture that many Christians have accepted can be paraphrased as follows: "OK, you have killed My prophets, stoned My messengers and rejected Me as your Messiah even though I have done miracles in your midst and spoken words that no man has performed or uttered since the world began, but I will eventually let you set up a secular state in this land and one day I will return to that state to establish My throne and will rule and reign in such Glory that you will all get saved."

To me, this reading is very different from what Jesus was actually saying. Jesus prophesies desolation for natural Israel and says in effect: "You had your chance to see a physical Messiah, to hug My neck, kiss My feet, hear My words first hand and view God in flesh form with your natural eyes. I made it easy for you. But now, because you reject me, your salvation will come when you receive the revelation that I have set up my habitation in My **sons** who will come to you in My Name, with My nature and My power wherever you live."

Unfortunately for all the Christians who look forward to seeing the physical Jesus, hugging His neck and kissing His feet, Jesus is saying here to the Jewish nation, and to all creation, that the day for that is over. Henceforth and forever, all people (Jew or Gentile) will get saved through the foolishness of preaching and by revelation of the Spirit. As Paul says in II Corinthians 5:16:

> Wherefore henceforth know we no man after the flesh: yea, though we have known Christ after the flesh, yet now henceforth know we him no more.

Christians have been so focused on a future physical coming of Jesus that they fail to see or appreciate the forest for the trees. His comings are multiple and more of a process of unfolding revelation within His people (at least within those that look for him) than an outward event. Glorious events will happen as more and more of His people come to the realization that unfortunately, a physical, glow-in-the-dark Jesus will not materialize in old Jerusalem to bail out (or replace, after we have sailed out) a weak and ineffectual Church that has fallen into apostasy.

The awesome and frightening truth is that the responsibility is on US to manifest Him in the earth, in Jerusalem, in Tehran, in Damascus, in New York City, and in every other corner of the world.

> And saviours shall come up on mount Zion to judge the mount of Esau; and the kingdom shall be the LORD's. Obad 21

The Doctrine of the Physical Return of Jesus

> But the hour cometh, and now is, when the true worshippers shall worship the Father *in spirit* and in truth: for the Father seeketh such to worship him. John 4:23

The Holy Spirit today is revealing the powerful truths of the kingdom of God to many in the Body of Christ. Revelation knowledge is increasing as more and more Christians come to the understanding that Christ and his kingdom are within us and that the fullness of the atoning work of Jesus is available to us right now. As many grow in spiritual understanding and faith, there remains an underlying misconception that prevents the people of God, even those who function in sonship ministries, from being conformed to the image of Christ.

It is the desire of the Father to raise up a people who can truly worship Him in Spirit and in Truth. When Jesus spoke these words to the Samaritan woman, He was pointing us away from our fleshly orientation that seeks a physical location and a physical person around whom to center our worship. He was pointing us away from the realm of the senses in order to reveal the dimension of the Spirit contained within the believer. This is why Jesus always pointed people to the Father during His ministry.

Jesus was the door to an invisible realm of Glory that we cannot fully enter into as long as we are focused on a physical Jesus who is now up in a place we call heaven but who will one day be walking the streets of Jerusalem. If you happen to live anywhere else, I guess you will be out of luck.

I say this to point out the absurdity of this notion that the Glory of God will one day be again localized in the physical body of Jesus Christ. The hope of Glory is not Christ sitting in a throne in Israel but Christ **in** us. All the scriptures that refer to the coming or appearance of Christ are based on a mistranslation of the Greek word *parousia* which means the presence or nearness. God's plan of the ages is to reveal Himself in His saints.

In order to accomplish this, the Father has to deliver us from our religious orientation which is geared to outward worship and to that which we can see with our eyes and handle physically. He wants to tear down our mansions in Glory Land and our dreams of kissing the nail-scarred hands of Jesus. God's people need to hear the Word of the Lord:

> Wherefore henceforth know we no man after the flesh: yea, though we have known Christ after the flesh, yet now henceforth know we him no more. II Cor 5:16

The transition from the old heaven, represented by Jesus' physical body, to the new heaven and the new earth, contained within the Church, has to occur in order to bring man back into spiritual fellowship with God through the indwelling of the Holy Spirit. The physical body of Jesus was the seed that had to **die** in order to bring about God's harvest – which is the manifestation of his Glory in a multi-membered body.

As long as that old heaven walked the earth, we could not come into our inheritance in God because the focus would always be on something outside of ourselves. If the Light of the world is *outside* ourselves, then darkness still reigns *within* us. As John the Baptist had to decrease that Jesus might increase, Jesus had to "go away" – He had to die and, after His resurrection, He had to ascend to the heavenlies no longer to walk the earth in His own physical body – so that the revelation of Himself **in us** might germinate and grow. That revelation of Himself in us is His "return" or "coming". Jesus gave His life to take away the old heaven that the new heaven in us might be established.

Will a man rob God? The "tithes and offerings" God wants in this day is the presentation of our bodies as a living sacrifice for His purposes. The doctrine of the physical return of Jesus, a pillar in the temple of carnal religion, robs God by reinforcing our reliance on the arm of flesh, even if that flesh belongs to Jesus. On a subtle level, a carnal doctrine will exert an influence on all aspects of our spiritual walk.

Because of this false religious doctrine, Christians are influenced – on a conscious or unconscious level – to rely on Jesus Christ to fully manifest the Glory of God. As a result, because of this misplaced hope and through ignorance of the plan of God, the people of God will never truly mortify their flesh or sow to the spirit. They may have all sorts of revelation truth, but as long as they are holding on to the physical body of Jesus and relying on His "coming," they have not in reality died to the flesh and death is at work in their own physical bodies.

Cast out the Bondwoman

> For this Agar is mount Sinai in Arabia, and answereth to Jerusalem which now is, and is in bondage with her children. But Jerusalem which is above is free, which is the mother of us all... But as then he that was born after the flesh persecuted him that was born after the Spirit, even so it is now. Nevertheless what saith the scripture? Cast out the bondwoman and her son: for the son of the bondwoman shall not be heir with the son of the freewoman. Heb 4:25-30

Throughout the history of the nation of Israel, there had been a wall of separation between Jews and Gentiles. God created this sense of separateness based on a shared history, natural genetics and a covenant relationship with Himself because it was pointing to the true wall of separation that would be unveiled with the advent of Jesus and the establishment of the Church. When the wall between Jews and Gentiles was torn down in Christ Jesus, the true separation was revealed to be – and in fact, in the mind of God, has always been – between the spiritual seed of God and the natural man.

One of most explosive verses in Paul's letters, explosive then and explosive now – if you have an ear to hear it – is Galatians 4:25 quoted above. I want to examine the implications of this verse and the 3 key reasons why it is so explosive.

The first reason is that it points to the fact that the history of Israel is allegorical. This means that although the events and people were factual and very real, they were all pointing to Christ and His Church. All the triumphant prophecies regarding Jerusalem or Israel in the Old Testament refer to the Church. This is not "replacement theology". The Church does not replace Israel. Israel was always a type or symbol of God's ultimate manifestation and that for which Jesus gave His life on Calvary: His glorious Church composed of Jew and Gentile. In admonishing a largely Gentile Church in Corinth, Paul writes the following:

> ...Now all these things happened unto them (referring to the children of Israel in the wilderness) for ensamples: and they are written for our admonition, upon whom the ends (goal) of the world (age) are come. I Cor 10:11

Secondly, in this verse, Paul makes the radical assertion that Hagar represents, not just the Arab people in the natural, but everyone who is bound by the law, including unconverted Jews and judaizing Christians, then and now. Sarah represents Christians – Jew or Gentile – who walk in the Spirit, not relying on nationality, genealogy, or the works of the law under the

Old Covenant but rather relying on faith and the grace of God which is no respecter of persons.

Thirdly, this verse points out that while most Christians are focused on a city in the Middle East, God's focus has always been on His heavenly Jerusalem or the Jerusalem that is above. The problem for most Christians is that they do not understand what "heavenly" refers to or what Paul meant by "above". In their carnal understanding, they locate this Jerusalem out in the clouds or in the afterlife when actually it is simply the Church which is God's spiritual Zion to which we are joined when we are born again (Heb 12:22). The natural Jerusalem is still in bondage along with all those (Jews, Christians and Moslems) who refuse to see the truth. They refuse to cast out the bondwoman, which interpreted means to make the distinction between flesh and Spirit and to choose the Spirit.

In focusing on the fleshly Israel and refusing to understand the Word by the Spirit, Christians are disenfranchising and disinheriting themselves from the promises of God, which is, of course, the aim of the enemy. When God tells us that our true citizenship is in His heavenly Jerusalem, why would we be obsessed with that which is below?

I guess it is much easier to put on a skullcap – metaphorically and literally, as in the case of some evangelicals who actually converted to Judaism – and celebrate Jewish holidays as so many Zionist Christians are doing today than to put on the mind of Christ and celebrate our new identity in Him where there is neither Jew nor Gentile.

Identity Theft

> Know ye not that ye are the temple of God, and that the Spirit of God dwelleth in you? I Cor 3:16

It is an interesting fact worth noting that everything in the realm of the natural is an expression of what is going on in the Church, that is, if you have ears to hear. There is no better example of this than the fears surrounding identity theft. Christians, like everyone else, are very concerned with guarding their identity from hackers and thieves. The irony of all this fear and caution is that, as far as Christians are concerned, the enemy has already hijacked, stolen and defrauded most of God's people of their true identity in Christ. Much attention is paid to the financial havoc created by someone stealing your social security number or ATM card while the real crime of spiritual identity theft goes undetected.

What do I mean by spiritual identity theft? Our spiritual journey can be seen as a progressive unfolding revelation of who He is in us and who we are in Him. This involves the forging of our spiritual identification with

Christ. The forging process starts with the knowledge and understanding of His eternal plan and the part we play in that plan. The identification is made a reality through His purifying fire that we gladly submit to because we have a vision of what is at stake. What the enemy seeks to do is to derail this process by locking us into the realm of spiritual ignorance and a carnal mindset that results in the loss of our spiritual identity and our full inheritance in Christ.

Over one hundred years ago the great English man of God, Andrew Jukes, lamented the spiritual ignorance of his generation of Christians. What was true then is even truer in our generation. Despite all the TV mega-ministries and worldwide evangelistic crusades, there is an appalling lack of spiritual understanding among God's people of who they are and what this is all about.

The spiritual identity theft that we see today has its roots in the early Church. We can see an example of this in the judaizing spirit that was taking hold of the Galatians. In this Church, Gentile Christians were beginning to see the simple gospel of grace that Paul had preached to them as somehow inadequate and looked to the Jewish law and religious rituals for their right standing with God. The enemy was skillfully undermining the work Paul had done to create in these new believers a spiritual understanding of God's eternal plan and their part in it.

In the Corinthian Church, the situation Paul encountered was quite different and yet the underlying problem was the same. It was a fellowship that was spiritually gifted but riddled with carnality, immaturity and divisiveness. Here, as in Galatia, the people of God were suffering from a loss of identity. In Corinth, however, the result was a lack of moral discipline and a loss of sanctifying faith rather than the legalism and works orientation that was threatening Galatia.

> Now all these things happened unto them for examples: and they are written for our admonition, upon whom the ends of the world are come. I Cor 10:11

> And what agreement hath the temple of God with idols? for ye are the temple of the living God; as God hath said, **I will dwell in them, and walk in them**; and I will be their God, and they shall be my people. II Cor 6:16

In the scriptures above we see Paul's remedy for the identity loss in Corinth and Galatia: a reminder that not only were Gentile believers equal with the children of Israel and as such, subject to the same severe disciplinary measures that Israel had to suffer in the wilderness, but that everything that happened to Israel in the Old Testament was for *their* benefit. It is the New Testament Church (Jew and Gentile, without distinction) "upon whom the ends (goal or point aimed at) of the world are come". Paul is saying (then and now): don't let the enemy rob you of the awareness of who you are and your high calling in Christ. Furthermore, do not let your carnality keep you from walking in your true identity in Him and from fulfilling that high calling.

Today we see both symptoms of identity theft on full display in the Church: the legalism and obsessive focus on natural Israel that threatened the Church in Galatia and all the carnality, worldliness and immaturity that characterized Corinth. We also see another interesting phenomenon. In order to restore our stolen spiritual identity, the Father is raising up voices proclaiming the message of the kingdom and the empowering revelation that God is truly in us. At the same time, however, the enemy is also raising up voices proclaiming a pseudo-kingdom message. These voices cater to the flesh of millions of Christians with a simplistic and superficial "kingdom" message that is little more than a feel-good band-aid to cover up the real need God's people have to understand who they are in Him. The enemy always promotes the cheap and easy way (the broad way) rather than the costly and hard way (the narrow way) that the preaching and teaching of the truth points us to.

I believe that it is this teaching and preaching that will educate, motivate and empower God's people to pay whatever price is required to be molded into the image of Christ as we seek our identity in Him.

Fasting: The Dethroning of Food

We live in an age and in a culture that are obsessed with food. We are surrounded by food magazines, restaurant blogs and cooking shows of every variety catering to every taste from diners and dives to haute cuisine. The Food Network has a vast audience and celebrity chefs have become cultural icons. As a recovering foodie myself, I can attest to the power this fascination with all things related to food can have over us. The problem is that this obsession has become a stronghold in God's people with disastrous results.

The fact that God's people have food issues is so obvious that all it takes is a glance at any congregation or gathering of Christians, especially in the US, to see the problem. I think statistics would confirm my view that obesity is a greater problem in the Church than it is in the world. The truth is that we use food in all kinds of ways that God never intended and that we are eating ourselves to death. We use it to comfort and console us, to reward us, to entertain us and to medicate us when we feel hurt, bored or stressed. We use it to compensate for other pleasures we feel deprived of. Instead of being a source of fuel and pleasure, we have gone overboard and have made food the center of many of our lives. We have transformed the temples of the Living God into toxic and defiled vessels. The Father has provided a powerful remedy to deliver us from this obsession which is the source of so many of the health problems of Christians. That remedy is fasting.

Now the subject of fasting is very controversial. The truth is that fasting is hard. After all, eating is one of the basic essentials of life. With the exception of breathing, it is the most essential factor of our physical existence. Fasting is no joyride but then again it is not meant to be. It is a sacrifice. But when we undertake that sacrifice to honor and obey God, He will honor and bless us. When you are divinely guided into a fast (and that is the key that I will get back to later), God will pour out His grace on you and He will make it possible for you to accomplish it. I have been on multiple day fasts where I felt no hunger pangs, no headaches and had no food fantasies. Truly, fasting can open the door to the realm of the supernatural.

Among other purposes it serves, fasting is God's way of bringing our fleshly appetites under submission to His Spirit. As long as we are in bondage to food, we cannot fully enter into the fullness of what He has ordained for us. It is very important to our spiritual growth and for that reason the enemy fights fasting with every weapon in his arsenal. I want to discuss a few of those weapons.

The most obvious weapon is fear which I will not dwell on for long. The cycle goes like this for many Christians: they abuse food, gain weight and then need to go on medication to control their sugar levels, blood pressure, heart disease and cholesterol. When God then tries to lead them into a fast, they are fearful of getting off their medication or that the fast will injure their compromised health. So we see that the enemy has Christians coming and going. He exerts his dominion through gluttony, disease, fear, unbelief, distrust and rebellion which all result in death.

The next weapon is less obvious and more hidden. I was having a friendly disagreement with a sister recently on the subject of fasting. She made the statement that Paul never mentions fasting in his epistles. I knew that he did but at the time could not recall the specific scriptural references.

When I got home, I did some studying and discovered something very interesting. The Strong's concordance (based on the King James translation) shows that Paul refers to fasting or fastings three times. The Young's Literal translation shows the same three references. However, when I checked seven other translations (the translations most commonly used by millions of Christians) there are no references to fasting or fastings in any of them in Paul's writings.

So in a way the sister was right. For two of the three references in the KJV (II Cor 6:5 and II Cor 11:27) where Paul is cataloging the hardships he had to endure for the sake of the Gospel, the seven other translations render the Greek word for fasting as hunger. The implication, which I think is somewhat valid, is that these were not voluntary fasts so much as circumstances where Paul was deprived of food.

Where my study got very interesting is with the third KJV reference in I Cor 7:5. This is the passage in which Paul is counseling married couples that it is acceptable to abstain from marital relations during times when they give themselves over to fasting and prayer. When I checked eight* other translations, each one had omitted the fasting part. The word was just altogether missing. There would seemingly be no justification for this omission because the word is clearly in the Greek original and the fasting referred to cannot be interpreted as forced like the other two references. For me, this has all the earmarks of a demonic conspiracy against fasting on the part of the translators. I don't know about you, but in my view, if the devil is against something to the point where he will deliberately alter the Word of God to eradicate a word, you should know that there is power in it.

The last weapon is also subtle and insidious. In the same conversation with this sister, I inquired about a couple we both know who I remembered as being really devoted to intensive fasting and intercessory prayer. I was wondering if they still fasted. Her response was that they no longer fasted because they are now eating raw foods. I said nothing at the time but as I thought about it later I began to see how really slick the enemy is. I have nothing against a raw food diet. In fact, I believe that God is leading His people in the direction of healthier eating including a diet of more raw food.

What I see the enemy doing, however, is replacing an obsession with unhealthy food with an obsession with healthy food. Christians spend much time and money on sustaining a vegetarian, vegan or raw food diet and some, apparently, feel that this regimen is a substitute for fasting. I believe that when God leads His people into a healthier diet, it is to make fasting easier, not to eliminate fasting. He wants to wean us from toxic, unhealthy food so that when we do fast we don't suffer from headaches and the other symptoms of food withdrawal.

I want to end this by saying that fasting should never be undertaken in the wrong spirit or with the wrong motive. It should not be undertaken in the spirit of religious asceticism nor should it be undertaken to change God's mind. We should fast in simple obedience to His leading believing that He will strengthen and sustain us for the duration of the fast. In order to do this, we need to hear His voice and to be sensitive to His leading. We cannot afford to take fasting off the table, so to speak, as many Christians seem to have done. In the coming months and years, we need to draw closer to Him than ever before and we need to have our inner man strengthened as we leave all bondages behind.

> I beseech you therefore, brethren, by the mercies of God, that ye present your bodies a living sacrifice, holy, acceptable unto God, which is your reasonable service. Rom. 12:1

*The Amplified Bible
 The Living Bible
 Phillips Modern English
 Revised Standard Version
 Today's English Version
 New International Version
 Jerusalem Bible
 New English Bible

The War Against the Second Birth

> Marvel not that I said unto thee, Ye must be born again. John 3:7

This is a startling declaration made by Jesus to Nicodemus in their nighttime encounter. The natural mind struggles, like Nicodemus, to make sense of this. How can we be re-born and more importantly, why would we need to be? In this teaching Jesus was inviting us to re-think what it means to be born, what our condition is at birth and presents to us a radical alternative: the second birth or the birth from above.

First let's look at what birth is. The birthing process is slow, painful and fraught with potential dangers for both mother and child. When the child finally emerges from the tight and dark confines of the birth canal, it enters an entirely new reality. The baby is fully engaged in receiving and interpreting information from this new world through his senses and later through the development of his rational mind. Millions of people have been born, live out their lives and die locked into this realm of the senses and of human reason without any idea that there exists another reality. Unfortunately, this includes many religious people or "masters of Israel" like Nicodemus.

Jesus was pointing him, and us, to the reality of another realm or dimension that we need to be born into to see or understand the kingdom of God. Just as an infant through much travail must leave the familiarity and comfort of the womb to enter an entirely new world, we too must break through into the realm of heaven through rebirth. Just as Jesus through His physical emergence from the womb of Mary took on the human condition and identity, through the second birth we take on the divine condition and identity. In doing this, we must leave behind everything associated with the first birth that contradicts, opposes or limits God and His purpose for us.

Let's look now at the first birth to see what the problem was that needed to be addressed by the second birth.

First Birth

> "Why do I need to be born again? I was born perfect the first time!" Facebook posting 2017

> "I was born this way and God doesn't make mistakes." Radio interview with a lesbian screenwriter

A theologian stated that the doctrine of original sin is the only Christian doctrine that is empirically verifiable. In other words, just look around you to see the confirmation that every man is born self-centered and indifferent to God, his creator. What seems to me and many others an obvious conclusion has actually been a topic of heated religious controversy for 2000 years.

The problem is that, by and large, people cannot seem to grasp or understand two seemingly contradictory ideas at the same time. So the people, historically, who believed that man was born in a sinful nature inherited from Adam very often had no understanding of, or faith in, the power of God to transform us through the second birth. They presented a very grim, pessimistic and ultimately demonic view of the Gospel. In fact, what exactly is the "good news" if we were born in sin and even after we are saved we continue to struggle with sin and can never be perfect in this life? (And those who reject this "Gospel" will be tormented in hell for all eternity. But that's the subject for another article...)

What we see today is a backlash against all that gloominess. Many teachers are declaring that we are born in a condition of slumber and need only be awakened by enlightened teaching. It is only our minds that have been brainwashed to believe that we are sinners. Jesus does repeatedly call for repentance or thinking anew but he also declares that the real change can only happen when we are born again, a much more radical prescription than "waking up" to treat a much more radical condition. Although Paul does not use the term "born again", he very insightfully points to the root of the problem of sin in chapter 7 of Romans. Sin is a <u>law</u> that is not just in our minds or our will but in our very members, our cell structure, our DNA. Sin is our Adamic inheritance.

Now let's look at the second birth so that we do not have to present to the world a gloomy "Gospel" or a watered-down cure to treat a watered-down disease.

The Second Birth

> And there appeared a great wonder in heaven; a woman clothed with the sun, and the moon under her feet, and upon her head a crown of twelve stars. And she being with child cried, travailing in birth, and pained to be delivered. And there appeared another wonder in heaven; and behold a great red dragon, having seven heads and ten horns, and seven crowns upon his heads. And his tail drew the third part of the stars of heaven, and did cast them to the earth: and the dragon stood before the woman which was ready to be delivered, for to devour her child as soon as it was born. Rev 12:1-4

You won't see all the forces of hell arrayed against a teaching or a revelation or a spiritual truth (as you see in the scripture above) unless it has the power to transform and conform lives into the very image of Christ. This is what is at stake here. Jesus was saying to Nicodemus that only by dying to everything associated with our carnal, sensual existence and being re-born into the dimension where He abided could we understand God or His kingdom. The truth of God comes from beyond this world.

As I have pointed to in the quotations above from popular culture and the theological see-saw regarding original sin, the warfare is very real. The need for a second birth is undermined by some modern Christian teachers but the general confusion and misunderstanding is compounded by institutional religion's deceptive teaching on what it is to be born again and how and when it happens. What Jesus was pointing to as a spiritual, individual and internal process, the religious system has succeeded in institutionalizing and externalizing.

As an example, the Catholic Church declares that the born again experience is conferred at baptism and reinforced at confirmation. We have this covered, they seem to say to millions of believers, no need for a personal relationship. I find it ironic that the Church that so vehemently opposes abortion in the natural has so much blood on its hands in aborting the second birth by preaching this deceptive doctrine. Religious hypocrisy has not changed in 2000 years.

On the other hand, Evangelicals, Charismatics and "Full Gospel" Churches equate salvation or coming to the alter with being born again. Anyone can respond to an alter call, sob profusely and go back to their pew unchanged. Many are baptized into water as a dry devil and come out of the water as a wet devil. When Peter declared that Jesus was the Son of God in response to the Master's question as to who He was, Peter made a declaration of the faith that saves. He was saved in his spirit man but was far from being born again. When you are just saved, like pre-Pentecost Peter, you can vacillate, back slide, fall away, get lukewarm, etc. The Peter we see on the day of Pentecost was not just saved but born again. When you are born again you cannot be unborn.

Am I equating being baptized with the Holy Spirit with being born again? Unfortunately, many who can speak in tongues or function in the other gifts of the Spirit are not born again. How do I know that? Jesus tells Nicodemus very clearly that he cannot see the kingdom of God unless he is born again. Millions of Charismatics are waiting for a so-called "second coming" instead of fully entering into the second birth. Many are waiting for God's kingdom to be established in the Middle East or are anticipating entering into the kingdom of God when they die or are raptured.

When you have been introduced into the heavenly kingdom by actually being birthed into it, you know that the kingdom of God or the kingdom of heaven (which are one and the same) is within you *by experience* and not just because you read it in the Bible or heard someone preach it to you. Your thoughts are transformed and your understanding is transformed. Those who are truly born again encounter more spiritual warfare from spirit-filled Christians than they do from anyone else. That says something profound and very revealing.

Conclusion

Now that hopefully we have some understanding of what it means to be born again and what it doesn't mean and the nature of the opposition, the question arises: why aren't we seeing more of a Christ-like manifestation in these born again sons of God? So many have dedicated their lives seeking to know God in His fullness, to understanding the mysteries of the kingdom and to conforming themselves to His image. They have encountered much opposition (internally and externally) in the process but have pressed into the kingdom through that straight and narrow birth canal. The problem is that many have one foot in the kingdom (second birth) and one foot in their fleshly identities, emotions, realities (first birth).

The primary symptom of this, as I see it, is the politicizing of the sons of God. Instead of drawing upon our identity as Christ in the earth from the realm and reality of the Spirit, we continue to cling to our human racial, national and political identities. Beloved, God is neither white nor black, neither American nor Canadian and neither Republican nor Democrat. We need to lose our tribal identities to take on the mind of Christ that transcends all those categories if we do not want to be guilty of idolatry.

When we allow the Spirit of God to root out of us all carnal identities and loyalties and when all our thoughts, emotions and actions are directed by the Spirit we can truly change this world. When we have experienced first hand the power of the second birth to establish us in our divine identity and to nullify everything associated with the Adamic first birth, we can effectively minister to that homosexual who declared that she was "born that way". We have the faith to declare that it doesn't matter how you were born, only that you get truly born again.

The Leaven of Herod

> And he charged them, saying, Take heed, beware of the leaven of the Pharisees, and *of* the leaven of Herod. Mark 8:15

In this verse Jesus was warning His disciples of a twofold danger to the Body of Christ that He knew would eventually become a snare and would lead to bondage and idolatry. These days Christians of almost every stripe are wary of the leaven of the Pharisees. There is a common understanding, a correct one I believe, that Jesus was pointing to legalistic and externalized forms of religiosity. Many Christians who consider themselves mature in their spiritual development have learned to recognize religious spirits and to discern false, man-made doctrines and teachings. Kingdom revelation abounds.

What doesn't abound and, in fact, what is rarely mentioned, taught or preached about is an understanding of the second caution: beware of the leaven of Herod. Very interesting. What is it and why is it a danger?

The answer to both questions is in the definition of Herod and in who he was. Herod was a political leader during the days of the ministry of Jesus. The name in Greek is Herodes and means "heroic". In His entire ministry, Jesus has only two very short teachings to His disciples on the subject of politics and they were both admonitions. This is one of them and the other is the famous "render unto Caesar" teaching.

His admonition against mixing our spirituality with worldly political agendas really goes to the heart of what it means to be born again or born from above. When our source of life, our thoughts and our very identity comes from the heavenly realm, there should be no room in our minds and in our emotions for the beggarly element of politics. Jesus knew that human political ideology had the power to divide His Body and to draw us into the realm of carnal identification with class, race, ethnicity, nationality and tribe that would undermine our unity in Christ and compromise our witness to a lost world. Moreover, all too often politics appeals to the ugliest human emotions: fear and hatred of those who are different, both of which call into question our love for others and our faith.

Regarding this undermined faith, I find it disturbing that so many Christians turn to a political agenda and seek worldly political power in the effort to advance some notion of restoring Godliness to our country. In my view, both the means and the motive are unbiblical. While Jesus mentions politics obliquely two times as warnings not to get entangled in that realm, Paul mentions it <u>once</u> with an exhortation for us to obey and pray for our leaders.

Understand that both Jesus and Paul lived in a Roman empire that was every bit as degenerate (if not more so) as our modern society. What disturbs and amazes me is that a supposedly born again, spirit filled Christian who recognizes and acknowledges that the source of his joy, his peace and his love is his relationship with Jesus Christ would offer up any other solution for the problems of others and the problems of society as a whole. Where is the recognition that the only real solution to every social problem is salvation and becoming a new creation? Do we place such a low value on our relationship with God? Or do we lack the faith that God is able, on a massive scale, to change so many lives that society itself changes? Legislation does not change hearts.

Jesus was looking to the future of His Church and seeing the danger that the new creation man would be pulled back into fear and unbelief through an obsession with and reliance on politics. He was seeing the division that would be created in His Body along racial lines. But the greatest danger He was seeing is the development of idolatry or hero worship in the hearts of his people (remember the definition of Herod?).

A few months ago, I saw a photograph taken at a Trump rally. One of the supporters in the picture was holding a sign that read: "Trump is our Savior". Beloved, no politician is our savior. No political party is the agent of God. No political agenda or program will convert hearts or radically change lives.

The Word of God declares that judgment begins in the house of God. Could it be that the changes we, as Christians, all long to see in society won't happen until we allow the judgment process to cleanse us of everything that is unlike God, including all forms of idolatry? When that truly happens, the sons of God will set the groaning creation free through love – not politics.

Laying the Axe to the Root

Then said he to the multitude that came forth to be baptized of him, O generation of vipers, who hath warned you to flee from the wrath to come? Bring forth therefore fruits worthy of repentance, and begin not to say within yourselves, We have Abraham to *our* father: for I say unto you, That God is able of these stones to raise up children unto Abraham. And now also the axe is laid unto the root of the trees: every tree therefore which bringeth not forth good fruit is hewn down, and cast into the fire. Luke 3:7-9

Thou *art* my battle axe *and* weapons of war: for with thee will I break in pieces the nations, and with thee will I destroy kingdoms; And with thee will I break in pieces the horse and his rider; and with thee will I break in pieces the chariot and his rider; With thee also will I break in pieces man and woman; and with thee will I break in pieces old and young; and with thee will I break in pieces the young man and the maid; I will also break in pieces with thee the shepherd and his flock; and with thee will I break in pieces the husbandman and his yoke of oxen; and with thee will I break in pieces captains and rulers. Jer 51:20-23

And like unto him was there no king before him, that turned to the LORD with all his heart, and with all his soul, and with all his might, according to all the law of Moses; neither after him arose there *any* like him. II Kings 23:25

Most Christians read the Old Testament, especially the books of Kings and Chronicles, as the history of the Israelite people. At best, they will detect foreshadowing of the Person and ministry of Jesus Christ. Very few Christians, however, read the accounts of the reigns of the kings of Israel as types (symbols) and shadows of their own lives and their own spiritual walk. When Peter tells us that we are priests and kings we tend not to make the connection with the kings that ruled Israel over 2000 years ago. I believe that we need to understand the reign of these kings, especially Josiah, to understand ourselves and what God wants from us.

In chapter 23 of II Kings we see a man of God on a holy rampage. He has caught sight of what God expects from His people and the revelation has caused him to tear up, root out, burn up and destroy every trace of idolatry in the land. The quotation above from Jeremiah, a contemporary of Josiah, contains the prophetic meaning of the actions taken in the natural by King Josiah. What does all this smashing, trashing, burning, pulling out by the roots have to do with us and why is it re-iterated in the New Testament? Let's examine this more closely.

We are born into this world with considerable baggage. According to Paul, we are born with an Adamic inheritance that corrupts every member of our body and distorts our very DNA. As we grow and develop, we acquire identities based on ethnic, racial and economic factors overlaid on our personality structures. We tend to identify with and be loyal to our tribe, our nation, our culture. We are taught to love our country and love our flag. We get emotional on hearing our national anthem. We develop political preferences and join parties, movements, etc. Those who get saved acquire the religious programming generated by their denomination. For many, this religious programming very often complements and reinforces the cultural programming they grew up with. If you are merely "saved" and not truly born again, your "Christianity" is cultural more than spiritual. You become part of the problem rather than part of the solution.

To be truly born again and to pursue God with a whole heart as Josiah did is to tear down every vestige of your carnal identity in order to take on the identity of Christ. It is to forsake one's loyalty to country, nationality, tribe or race. We are to be neither male nor female, Jew nor Gentile, free nor slave. We are to be neither Democrat nor Republican. We are neither American nor Canadian. We are citizens of another country.

So many Christians who claim to be born again, spirit-filled sons of God continue to draw their identities and thoughts from the realm of carnality. They have allowed themselves to be seduced by political manipulators and compromised by worldly agendas. In the effort to force their ideas on others and in the effort to get unsaved people to behave as though they were saved,

Christians have corrupted themselves in the pursuit of political power. For many Christians, the end justifies the means. When that end seems to be frustrated, they see conspiracies on every hand and the "opposition" is demonized.

In truth, Christians have only one enemy. That enemy is not Democrats, not liberals, not the "deep state". That enemy is Satan. And he is apolitical. The current obsession with conspiracies is ironic because the <u>true</u> conspiracy is Satan's (very successful) effort to keep born again Christians out of the second birth and into the carnalities of the first birth. He wants to keep us from fully walking in our spiritual identity as Christ. He wants to compromise our witness in the earth by attaching us to political ideologies that are often hateful, corrupt and even racist. He wants to divide the Body of Christ along racial and political lines.

Beloved, idolatry of any kind is hated by God and He will uproot it even if He has to take us to the grave so it can be dealt with in the spirit realm. It's instructive to note that despite God's approval of Josiah's zeal and despite His promise that Josiah would die in peace, Josiah did not die in peace. Against the warning of God, Josiah got involved in a worldly conflict that he had no business getting involved in. He took sides in a battle that did not concern him. He decided to eat from the Tree of the knowledge of Good and Evil instead of the Tree of Life. Josiah declared one side "good" and the other side "evil" and sided with the "good" team. In so doing, he dug his own grave.

Josiah, like each of us, was called to pull down the idols in his own heart, to cleanse the house of God that had been polluted by paganism and worldliness and to prepare God's people to become the manifestation of Himself in the earth.

Through The Veil

It is the glory of God to conceal a thing: but the honour of kings is to search out a matter…

Cana

Transformative Word:
Marriage of spirit and flesh.
He the host, He the bride, He the groom,
He the water, He the wine,
He the metaphor divine.

The Rent Veil

For the Church, everything we need to know about who we are and where we are in the eyes of God is contained in the physical layout of the tabernacle. The crucial significance of the rending of the veil that separated the Holy Place from the Most Holy Place is apparently misunderstood by so many Christians judging by the unscriptural doctrines that pass for orthodoxy. Let us look at that rent veil and the profundity of what it signifies for God's people.

Up until the crucifixion of Jesus, the people of God, symbolized by the golden candlestick in the Holy Place, were separated from the ark and mercy seat in the Most Holy Place that typified or represented the presence of God and His throne in the heavenly realm. The two chambers were separated by a veil embroidered with cherubim. This veil stood for the physical body of Jesus Christ which, during His earthly ministry, both illuminated the glory of God for those anointed to see it and veiled it off. At His crucifixion, the veil in the temple in Jerusalem was split in two to signify that the purpose of God was accomplished for that physical body.

This means that the Church on earth is now in the same room as the throne of God. A mighty new reality was created for believers which is described in Hebrews 12:22-24. Old Jerusalem and her children are now superseded by the New Jerusalem and her children, the sons of God, Jew and gentile. Everything that had been natural and physical is now spiritual and heavenly while still on earth.

What we see in the history of the Church is an apostasy that sews back the veil creating a distortion in the Gospel. The glorious reality that Jesus opened up to us has been closed off through the doctrines of men that center on the physical body of Jesus. These doctrines have believers focused on a desire to see Jesus in physical form either at the so-called rapture, or in old Jerusalem or in that place they call heaven. They want to see Jesus anywhere but in the mirror.

The Father has revealed to me that one of the sad consequences of this unscriptural focus on the physical man Jesus is that it limits the scope of outreach. The images of Jesus conjured up by most Western Christians have been of a European-looking white man with flowing chestnut hair. Just check out every piece of art depicting Christ from the Middle Ages to the popular image hanging on the walls of many Christians' homes.

I am not trying to make the point that the historic Jesus instead had Semitic features (which He most certainly did have), but rather that Jesus Christ is now a Spirit man who is physically manifested in the flesh bodies of the full color spectrum of saved humanity. I know for a fact that many African Americans have converted to Islam because they reject a Christianity which focuses on the adoration of a white man. How many people turn to Islam, Buddhism, New Age or the occult for this same reason?

The question I have been asked regarding the Spirit man Christ Jesus is what happened to the flesh body of Jesus? Was it not resurrected? What the Spirit has shown me is that the physical structure that the disciples knew and loved was taken over by the resurrection power contained in Jesus' inner man. Jesus, in that sense, was resurrected bodily but He was released from His identification with that one particular physical body in order to be able to inhabit, by the Spirit of resurrection, the physical bodies of each and every one of His sons, we who are the children of the resurrection. In other words, the physical body that walked the shores of Galilee had served its purpose and was no longer the exclusive habitation of the Holy Ghost.

Christians who struggle with this need to ask themselves why the resurrected Jesus seemed to make it a point to appear in bodies that were unrecognizable to His disciples. He did this in the garden, He did this on the road to Emmaus, and He did it on the shore of Galilee as He prepared breakfast. (When He did appear with the wounds of the crucifixion, it was merely to help their unbelief.) Some have concocted theories that He was so illuminated that the disciples could not see His face. Really?

The truth is that He was bringing home to them the reality that henceforth they were not to know Him by the flesh but by the Spirit. He was saying: "Don't look for that body you knew in Galilee. I have a new body. Yours!"

"Christ in you, the hope of glory..." Col 1:27

Enduring Faith

"Oh the delivering power of a vision big enough,
heavenly enough, divine enough to swallow up all
of our petty and personal interests!"
T. Austin-Powers

I recently heard a comment by a speaker that did not sit well in my spirit. The speaker was exhorting his listeners to rise to a greater level of faith. I was in full agreement with that until he made the observation that all the faith we muster on this side will be gratified when we "get to heaven" where faith will no longer be needed. I think that this is a notion that is commonly held by most Christians and is in fact the underpinning of much fundamentalist and evangelical theology. It is part of the basic salvation scenario that is unexamined by most people. But is it true?

It is certainly not true of those heroes of faith named in the "hall of fame" described in chapter 11 of Hebrews. We really need to ponder the implications of this chapter and the following chapter, especially

Hebrews 12:1. For these righteous ones, passing into "heaven" did not mean an end of their faith. We need to ask ourselves why their attention is focused on us, the Church here on earth. Their focus is actually on a City and, unlike most Christians today, the City they are focused on is the New Jerusalem (that's us!) and not on the Old Jerusalem which is in bondage along with all her children (Jew, Moslem and Christian).

What explains this focus? The reason is that again, unlike most Christians, these saints have come to understand the fullness of God's thoughts and the scope of His plan for the Church here on earth. His passion has become their passion and like Him, they are looking for a people in this realm who share that passion, a people who know who they are in Christ and who are pressing into perfection. These saints in the spirit realm need an enduring faith that the great plan of God will one day be manifested in a body of overcomers in this physical realm.

Do not make the mistake of assuming that the cloud of witnesses described in Hebrews is only composed of Old Testament saints. If you envision Paul sitting out there somewhere by the River of Life enjoying the heavenly scenery, you do not understand Paul or God. Paul – like the other New Testament writers, as well as every saint since then – is invested in us and in our journey toward attaining the fullness of the stature of Christ which he preached about.

You see, it is all about the Church here on earth coming into perfection. Christians really need to let go of their selfish individualism, their carnal imagery concerning the spirit realm and their emotional attachment to earthly Old Jerusalem and man-made doctrines. Like Abraham and like Paul, we need an overcoming faith that even death cannot destroy.

Emmanuel

Behold, a virgin shall be with child, and shall bring forth a son, and they shall call his name Emmanuel, which being interpreted is, God with us. Matt 1:23 (KJV Translation)

'Lo, the virgin shall conceive, and she shall bring forth a son, and they shall call his name Emmanuel,' which is, being interpreted 'With us [he is] God.' Matt 1:23 (Young's Literal Translation)

I was struck by the Young's Literal translation and how it provides a powerful insight into God's plan for the ages, if you think about it for awhile. With us, He is God. This is not to say that without us He is not God. But I believe that by creating man and the physical dimension in which we live, God intended to magnify and enlarge His Godship. How is He doing this? Through the revelation in this dimension of His Son, the man Christ Jesus, and through the unfolding and unveiling of His multi-membered Body. And the amazing thing (if you have ears to hear it) is that the fall of Adam actually makes that enlargement possible and was all part of His plan.

If you have a problem with that last statement, please consider the fact that Jesus was the Lamb that was slain from the foundation of the world. In other words, before Adam ever sinned, God had made provision for the reconciling of the creation back to Himself through the blood of the Lamb. This is what Paul was referring to in Romans 8:20-21 when he speaks of the creation being made subject to vanity (through the fall of Adam) not willingly but because God ordained it to accomplish His purpose. The purpose in letting the creation fall to the depths of degradation and depravity was to prove to the powers and principalities that are watching all this unfold that God's love is powerful enough to be able to reach into the lowest depths to bring radical transformation and reconciliation. Without the fall, how would we ever understand His grace?

We see a dramatic demonstration of the unfolding of God's plan in the events on the day of Pentecost. What happened on the day of Pentecost is that the Godhead - Father and Son - incorporated into themselves, through the Holy Spirit, the followers of Jesus who were gathered in the Upper Room. Later that day, 3000 people from all nations responded to the preaching of Peter and were also incorporated into the Godhead. On that glorious day, God was able to manifest Himself in flesh form as never before in 3120 people. And that was just the start.

The awesome truth is that we are His Glory and He desires to be seen in us, through us and as us. In this way, in effect, He expands His Godship as every shred of opposition in fallen man has been, is being and will be overcome. This is why He is called the Lord God Almighty that was, that is and that is to come. It is through this expansion of His dominion over a rebellious creation that He will become all in all. And this is what the progressive revelation of His kingdom is all about.

Unless a Seed Die:
The Mystery of the Third Heaven

> But some man will say, How are the dead raised up? And with what body do they come? Thou fool, that which thou sowest is not quickened, except it die: And that which thou sowest, thou sowest not that body which shall be, but bare grain...But God gives it a body as it hath pleased him, and to every seed his own body. I Cor 15:35-38

Since the fall of Adam, the carnal mind of man has been oriented to worship a localized and external God, usually one associated with a physical building or located way out beyond the blue. God, on the other hand, wants to enter into a union with man that is so intimate that we take on His identity and His character and our physical body becomes His physical body.

To accomplish this, God had to take the creation through a teaching process in which man is being slowly weaned from worship centered around outward things to internal spiritual worship. God does this by taking man through a succession of heavens or manifestations of His

Glory. Before I discuss the three manifestations of God's Glory that He has unveiled to man, we need to look at the reason for man's focus on the outward.

We tend to view the casting out of Adam from the Garden of Eden as a "Fall" or downward spiritual movement or, if our thoughts are on a more carnal plane, as a movement out of one location on earth to a less desirable location. The expulsion actually involved a change in man's focus from the internal paradise of God where he enjoyed continual fellowship with his Creator to a focus on the external world of the senses. This is the world where human intellect and the soulish emotions reign supreme. They reign supreme because the throne in man that was once occupied by God is now occupied by man's carnal intellect which is the antichrist, that man of sin who opposes God by seeking to always keep God outside of man.

It has been God's plan since the Fall to return man to the paradise of internal spiritual fellowship, which is heaven, by unfolding the heavenly realm in three stages. When God finished with one heaven, or revelation of His Glory, He was ready to move on to the next heaven and woe unto those saints who do not move with Him! This is why the scripture speaks of the destruction of the heavens ("For my sword shall be bathed in heaven..." Isa 34:5), or the heavens changing and waxing old as a garment (Heb 1:10-11), or the heavens passing away with a great noise (II Peter 3:10).

The first heaven was contained in the tabernacle in the wilderness. It was here that God first manifested His Glory in the midst of His called out people. This heaven, even though it was external to man and housed in a physical structure, contained the pattern and foreshadowing of the greater revelation to come.

Man's carnal intellect had no problem with the first heaven, but all hell broke loose when God unveiled the second heaven or the physical body of Jesus Christ. The spirit of antichrist which is within man hates the truth that the Glory of God can be contained in a physical body. It goes against the grain of the religious mentality and was seen as blasphemy by those, then and now, still inhabiting the first heaven. As radical as the revelation of the second heaven was, the carnal mind could still take comfort in the reality that the second heaven was external to man and localized, being confined to one physical body. Christianity could spread over the entire globe and the spirit of antichrist would be relatively unfazed as long as the focus remained on the historical Jesus of the past or the glorified Jesus of the future. Either way, the kingdom of the antichrist within man is untouched.

If the ushering in of the second heaven in the form of the manifestation of God in the individual body of Jesus caused hell to break loose, how much more the manifestation of the third heaven: an army of messiahs each one containing the fullness of the Godhead – Father, Son and Holy Ghost! The Church world now has no problem with the second heaven – the Glory contained in one body 2000 years ago or in a glorified Jesus to be encountered in the afterlife or in the "rapture". But the spirit of antichrist that rules this religious world will fight tooth and nail against the revelation of the third heaven. Why? Because the carnal intellect of man does not want to surrender the throne and be replaced by the mind of Christ. And so the vast majority of Christians are either hung up on the historical Jesus or waiting for Him to appear in the clouds or to meet Him at death.

The transition from the second heaven to the third heaven has to occur in order to bring man back into spiritual fellowship with God through the indwelling of the Holy Spirit. The physical body of Jesus was the seed that had to **die** in order to bring about God's harvest – which is the manifestation of His Glory in a multi-membered body. As long as that second heaven walked the earth, we could not come into our inheritance in God because the focus would always be on something outside of ourselves. If the Light of the world is outside ourselves, then darkness still reigns within us. As John the Baptist had to decrease that Jesus might increase, Jesus had to "go away" – He had to die and, after His resurrection, He had to ascend to the heavenlies no longer to walk the earth in His own physical body – so that the revelation of Himself in us might germinate and grow.

That revelation of Himself in us is His "return" or "coming". Jesus gave His life to take away the old heaven that the new heaven in us might be established. When He paid such a price to open up the revelation of the third heaven, it grieves His Spirit that Christians persist in hanging on to the second heaven by putting their hopes on the reappearance of Jesus in His own individual physical body.

Some Christians try to have it both ways. They halt between two opinions by trying to have their cake and eat it, too, so to speak. They understand that the sons of God will manifest the fullness of God's Glory but they believe that at the end of the age, Jesus will appear to head the army of glorified sons. The second heaven in glorified form will make a second appearance. The problem is that as soon as the Glory of God is again localized and externalized (and believe me, if Jesus in physical form headed an army consisting of you and me, all focus would be on Him) all sorts of carnal absurdities arise. Christians would trample each other to be physically close to this physical Jesus.

The truth of the matter is that the re-introduction of the second heaven in the form of the separate physical body of Jesus would nullify the third heaven. The sons of God would become the "2nd class" Body of Christ overshadowed by his "real" individual body. The veil of the tabernacle that was rent, which represented his individual flesh body, would be sewn back up and the Glory of God once again kept at a distance from us.

The scripture that is cited to support the physical return of Jesus is the passage in Acts 1:11 where the angel asked the disciples why they were looking to the sky for the return of Jesus.

> Ye men of Galilee, why stand ye gazing up into heaven? This same Jesus, which is taken up from you into heaven, shall so come in like manner as ye have seen him go into heaven.

The angel here is speaking a prophetic utterance using God's spiritual language which cannot be interpreted literally. Just like the men of Galilee, Christians today are still looking to the sky for the return of Jesus. The same Jesus that was received and hidden from the view of His disciples by a literal cloud in a physical sky, appeared in like manner to the disciples in the Upper Room, to John on the island of Patmos and to many of us as the Father began revealing the truths of the kingdom message. His unveiling is in "like manner" except that the natural has now become spiritual: now He is unveiled as the Sun of righteousness breaking through the Glory Cloud containing myriads of saints.

The have-it-both-ways theology of many Christians who still inhabit the revelation of the second heaven contradicts the truth that we are truly bone of His bone and flesh of His flesh. Unlike physical marriage where each partner retains his or her own identity and body, the mystical union of Christ and the Church produces a new creation which is the flesh regenerated and inhabited by the spirit of Christ. In this true union, there is now no longer two but just one. This is why Jesus said in Matt 23:29: "...ye shall not see me henceforth, till ye shall say, Blessed is he that cometh in the name of the Lord." The only way to see Him in the future will be to see Him in His sons.

The sons of God are the Body of Christ in a two-fold sense: we are members of the collective, multi-membered body and we are each individually His body. The spirit of antichrist allows Christians to believe that they are members of the collective Body of Christ but will not allow them to really believe, beyond lip-service, that their own body is truly His body because, on some level, they are still hanging on to the physical Jesus.

Just as Jesus' individual physical body, as the seed of the glorified multi-membered body, needed to die to bring forth the Church, we need to die to our carnal attachment to that seed body, or second heaven, and we need to awaken to the knowledge that **we are His only physical body**. When this truly happens, the Glory of God can be seen not in one body but in every body as the third heaven unfolds and as we enter that place in God, and indeed, become that place in God where Paul heard those unspeakable words that could not be uttered in his day.

The Land of Milk and Honey

> Look down from thy holy habitation, from heaven, and bless thy people Israel, and the land which thou hast given us, as thou swarest unto our fathers, a land that floweth with milk and honey. Deut 26:15

> In the day that I lifted up mine hand unto them, to bring them forth of the land of Egypt into a land that I had espied for them, flowing with milk and honey, which is the glory of all lands...Eze 20:6

God made a precious promise to Abraham that one day his heirs would be the possessors of a land that flowed with milk and honey. We can also see, throughout scripture, the promise that the people of God would inherit the earth. It is important to understand that the Old Testament is filled with types (symbols) and shadows of a greater spiritual reality. What then was the land of milk and honey pointing to? What earth is it that the meek will inherit? It might be helpful first to discuss what these promises were not referring to.

Not Geographic

> By faith Abraham, when he was called to go out into a place which he should after receive for an inheritance, obeyed; and he went out, not knowing whither he went. By faith he sojourned in the land of promise, as in a strange country, dwelling in tabernacles with Isaac and Jacob, the heirs with him of the same promise: For he looked for a city which hath foundations, whose builder and maker is God...These all died in faith, not having received the promises, but having seen them afar off, and were persuaded of them, and embraced them, and confessed that they were strangers and pilgrims on the earth. Heb 11:8-10,13

As we can see in the above scripture, Abraham was physically in the geographic location that his heirs would one day be occupying after their sojourn in Egyptian bondage. But Hebrews tells us that by faith he received the revelation that the promise of God would not be fulfilled in a physical parcel of land, however beautiful, in the Middle East. He saw that the fulfillment would be seen in a body of people, a City of God, that would not be unveiled in his lifetime and that had no connection to a geographic location.

While Abraham had this revelation, the literal and physical types (symbols) had to be enacted by his heirs in order to create a pattern in the natural of spiritual reality. The experiences of the children of Israel, Abraham's natural heirs, were to be examples for the

Body of Christ. So in the process of time, the children of Israel fell into Egyptian bondage and were delivered by Moses into the promised land of milk and honey through much struggle and travail. In the years that followed, the land was polluted with the rebellion and idolatry of the Israelites because, after all, it was just a type (symbol) and shadow of something that cannot be polluted.

> Jesus saith unto her, Woman, believe me, the hour cometh, when ye shall neither in this mountain, nor yet at Jerusalem, worship the Father. Ye worship ye know not what: we know what we worship: for salvation is of the Jews. But the hour cometh, and now is, when the true worshippers shall worship the Father in spirit and in truth: for the Father seeketh such to worship him. God is a Spirit: and they that worship him must worship him in spirit and in truth. John 4:21-24

Looking at this passage we see an aspect of the ministry of Jesus that is seldom taught or preached in pulpits today. Here we see Jesus dismantling the focus on physical geography that held in bondage the Jews of that day and so many Christians today. This scene with the Samaritan woman is shocking and revelatory.
It was shocking because Jews did not interact with Samaritans. Jewish rabbis did not converse at the watering hole with women of possible ill-repute. But the most shocking and revelatory part, for those with ears to hear, is the manner in which Jesus demolished our human, carnal attachment to locality or geography. God was here declaring that He is finished with geography, "holy lands", sacred spaces or any understanding of the "promised land" as something outward.

Not in the Afterlife

> And these all, having obtained a good report through faith, received not the promise: God having provided some better thing for us, that they without us should not be made perfect. Heb 11:39-40

At this point you might be thinking, as many Christians do, that the land of milk and honey is a reference to "heaven" or the afterlife. But if you carefully consider the above scripture from Hebrews, a question arises. If these heroes of faith were already in the spirit realm or the afterlife or "heaven", why were they looking to us (and are even now looking to us), the Body of Christ on the earth, for the fulfillment of the promise given to Abraham and the children of Israel in the wilderness?

> Brethren, I count not myself to have apprehended: but this one thing I do, forgetting those things which are behind, and reaching forth unto those things which are before, I press toward the mark for the prize of the high calling of God in Christ Jesus...Who shall change our vile body, that it may be fashioned like unto his glorious body, according to the working whereby he is able even to subdue all things unto himself. Phil 3:13-14 & 21

It is apparent from the above scriptures that Paul was not striving to enter the afterlife. Entering the afterlife, or "heaven" as most Christians conceive it, was not the mark of the high calling in Christ Jesus. What goal was it then that Paul was pressing toward but never attained in his lifetime?

Looking again at the types (symbols) and shadows that the children of Israel enacted for our benefit, we see some clues and parallels. First, we see that the key element was faith. Going into the afterlife for these children of Israel in the wilderness was not a reward but a punishment for unbelief. The promised land of milk and honey was entered into through faith under the leadership of Joshua (a type of Jesus). They had to be circumcised and to pass through the River Jordan (a type of death to our human, carnal way of thinking).

The second clue is the fact that the land of Canaan was not uninhabited. In fact, the children of Israel had enemies on every side that had to be conquered through battle and faith in that mighty Man of War that led them.

What then is the reality that these parallels, these types and shadows point us to? What then is the land that is totally pleasing to God, the earth that He wants us to inherit? That promised land is our physical bodies that have been redeemed in full and in which, through an overcoming faith and obedience to our leader, Christ Jesus, all enemies have been conquered and defeated, the last enemy, of course, being death. This is what those heroes of faith in the cloud of witnesses, including Abraham and Paul, are waiting to see. This is what the whole creation is groaning to see manifested.

> I will ransom them from the power of the grave; I will redeem them from death: O death, I will be thy plagues; O grave, I will be thy destruction... Hosea 13:14

The Spiritual Roots of Homosexuality

> Because that, when they knew God, they glorified him not as God, neither were thankful: but became vain in their imaginations, and their foolish heart was darkened. Professing themselves to be wise, they became fools, and changed the glory of the uncorruptible God into an image made like to corruptible man, and to birds, and four-footed beasts, and creeping things. Wherefore God also gave them up to uncleanness through the lusts of their own hearts, to dishonor their own bodies between themselves: who changed the truth of God into a lie, and worshipped and served the creature more than the Creator, who is blessed forever. Amen. Rom 1:21-25

We see in these verses that both sexual perversion and idolatrous religion have their roots in the rebellion of the creation against the Creator. As soon as man turned his back on his Creator, he began a perverted love affair with the creation. This spiritual perversion began to manifest in the natural as sexual perversion. Man's rebellion against God resulted in an arrested development that can be seen in both spiritual and sexual manifestation. It is for this reason that there is such a strong affinity between homosexuality and the spirit of religion and why the churches are filled with homosexuals in need of a message and an anointing that will deliver them. Let us examine the relationship between spiritual and sexual perversion.

The Sexual Types

> For this cause God gave them up unto vile affections: for even their women did change the natural use into that which is against nature.
> Rom 1:26

The first description given in this passage from Romans is of female homosexuality because lesbianism is a type of, or represents, the first level of deception found in the Babylonian religious system. Many Christians who are members of mainline churches have failed to come into proper relationship with Christ as their head. These dead denominational churches that had their origins and roots in genuine revivals of the Holy Spirit today are nothing more than social clubs or forums for political correctness. The headship of Jesus Christ is either not acknowledged at all or given merely lip service.

God intended the Church or Body of Christ, as His female, to be united to Jesus Christ as the Bride is joined to the Bridegroom. Lesbianism is symbolic of churches (females) or Christians who reject the Bridegroom. The system's rejection of the leadership of the Man or Christ is seen as spiritual lesbianism by God because the creation, which is considered female in the mind of God, worships and serves itself rather than the Creator.

> And likewise also the men, leaving the natural use of the woman, burned in their lust one toward another; men with men working that which is unseemly, and receiving in themselves that recompense of their error which was meet. Rom 1:27

The second level of deception, represented by male homosexuality, is more subtle than the first. Here the enemy mixes just enough truth with the lie so that the bondage (both sexual and spiritual) runs deep. Male homosexuality is a type of, or represents, those Christians who have come to the basic revelation that the Church is the Bride and that Christ is the Bridegroom to whom we are united in bonds of love. These Christians have the revelation that they are the female united to the male but all spiritual progress stops there. The system resists, rejects and rebels against the revelation that we are Christ and that we possess all that He possesses.

In the psychological and sexual development of a male child, he begins life identifying with his mother exactly as a little girl does. However at a certain age, in the normal development of the boy, he must begin to pull away from his mother and begin identifying with the male parent in order to learn what it is to be a man and how to relate to females as a male. If that transition from identifying with the female to identifying with the male is never made, the boy's development is arrested and psychological and sexual problems manifest.

In the spiritual parallel, to move into the fullness of the stature of Christ is to step out of the female aspect of

God (the Bride) into the male aspect (Sonship) for the purpose of ministry or spiritual reproduction. Many Christians reject sonship, resist the message of the kingdom and refuse to grow into a mature identity with the man Christ Jesus. Instead of becoming conformed to His image and growing "unto a perfect man, unto the measure of the stature of the fullness of Christ: that we henceforth be no more children...", they would rather relate to Jesus as a female in the same way that a homosexual man desires to relate to men in a feminine mode rather than asserting and identifying with his own masculinity.

The Spiritual Reality

> Even as Sodom and Gomorrha and the cities about them in like manner giving themselves over to fornication, and going after strange flesh... Jude 7

In this passage Jude is comparing spiritual rebellion with the sexual sins of Sodom and Gomorrah. These sins, fornication and going after strange flesh, must be seen in a spiritual light to get the deeper meaning and to understand the spiritual parallel. In spiritual application, the "strange flesh" is actually the flesh of Jesus.

Like the homosexual who is so deceived about who he is or what he already has, the religious system of man has deceived Christians into desiring fellowship with the flesh of Jesus instead of presenting their bodies a living sacrifice in order to become His flesh. Jesus gave His disciples the commandment to eat His flesh in order that it be digested, that His flesh would become our flesh, not "strange" flesh. It is their attachment to the "strange" flesh of Jesus that has so many Christians in bondage and that keeps them in spiritual immaturity.

Another powerful scripture that shows the connection between sexual perversion and spiritual rebellion is found in the book of Revelation:

> And their dead bodies shall lie in the street of the great city, which spiritually is called Sodom and Egypt, where also our Lord was crucified. Rev 11:8

Where also our Lord was crucified. What does this mean? We see in this scripture that, in the mind of God, Sodom and the sins of the Sodomites have a spiritual significance that has nothing to do with sexuality. It was not homosexuals that crucified Jesus but rather the old pharisaical order. The sexual manifestation is merely an outward sign of something much more offensive to God: the religious system of man (Judaic in Jesus' day and now Christian in our day). God has compassion on homosexuals. God's wrath is aimed at the spiritual homosexuals that populate the "great city" referred to in this passage. That city is the Jerusalem that is "below" or in the realm of carnality which Paul contrasts with spiritual Jerusalem that is "above" (Gal 4:25-26).

In the mind of God, the Jerusalem that is below is spiritually synonymous with the whore, Babylon, and as we can see here, with Sodom and Egypt. They all speak of a place where God's people are held in bondage - not to secular authority but to fleshly religious authority and to their own attachment to that authority. They also speak of a place that will crucify those who, like Jesus, proclaim the truths of God's kingdom.

While the religious system makes an attempt to minister to homosexuals and to get them delivered, the success is sporadic because it is an example of the blind leading the blind. There can be no dramatic and massive deliverance until the underlying spiritual causes of homosexuality are recognized and judged within the Church. Cleansing and judgment must begin in the household of God. If the Church is to minister in power and compassion to homosexuals, Christians must repent of the unscriptural teachings and judgmental spirits that have hindered their effectiveness. Indeed, the only hope for the Church and for all creation lies in the preaching of the kingdom message and in the unveiling of the sons of God:

> Because the creature itself also shall be delivered from the bondage of corruption into the glorious liberty of the children of God. Rom 8:21

When the sons of God begin to manifest, all aspects of man's rebellion and the fruit of that rebellion will be reversed as the Sun of righteousness arises within us with healing in His wings.

The Doctrine of Death

> If a man keep my saying, he shall never see death.
> John 8:51

The statements of Jesus concerning eternal life were so startling to the hearers of His day that they thought Him insane and dangerous and sought to kill Him. We must ask ourselves why His words concerning eternal life provoked such a response. This violent reaction is in marked contrast to the way in which Christians today receive His words. As a result of 2,000 years of religious programming and false teaching, Christians today interpret Jesus' words in a way that nullifies and robs them of their power.

What we see reflected in the theologies of all Christian denominations is the common sense understanding which declares: "He could not have meant physical death because, after all, everybody dies". Thus begins the process whereby the powerful statements of faith proclaimed by the Word of God – and there is no statement more powerful than the promise that believers can overcome death – are interpreted in light of the collective experience of Christians who were never exposed to the truth. Christians die because the necessary precondition for conquering death, which is an overcoming faith, is not encouraged and then the fact that Christians die just like unbelievers is used, in turn, to justify the doctrine of death.

The religious system, which God calls Babylon in the book of Revelation, teaches that immortality applies after we experience a physical death and relates basically to an afterlife. This makes the concept of immortality contradictory, if not absurd. Paul tells us that Jesus Christ was manifested to *abolish* death and to bring life and immortality to light. If immortality becomes effectual after we die, why did Jesus need to bring it to light? To the Hebrew people, there would have been nothing radical about the proclamation of an afterlife – certainly nothing that would produce scandal, shock and provoke persecution.

If the Father, through Jesus, was merely ushering in a new, glorified after-life for believers as the system teaches in its interpretation of the scripture: "O Death, where is thy sting?", why does the writer of the book of Hebrews describe the heroes of faith in the Old Testament and then go on to say that this cloud of witnesses surrounds believers in the flesh looking to us in the here and now to bring them into perfection (Heb. 11 and 12)? This tells me that the focus of the saints in the spirit realm is on the saints who are still in their physical bodies. Why? They are looking to us to accomplish in the flesh that which they could not attain to in their lifetimes – victory over death.

If the ministry of Jesus was to cleanse us from sin so that, after we die, we can enjoy eternity with God, why was He the Passover Lamb? The blood of the Passover lamb in the Old Testament was a covering to protect the children of Israel from the angel of death and was a type of Jesus' true ministry: to deliver us from death, in all its forms, by delivering us from sin.

Death Enthroned

While Jesus came to deliver the creation from the bondage of death and corruption, the goal of the enemy working through the Babylonian religious system of man is to keep believers in the shadow of darkness where death reigns. Not only are the common sense assumptions of the carnal mind ("everybody has to die") never challenged by the teachings of the religious system, they are, in fact, reinforced. Christianity, in all its various forms and manifestations, accepts and even glorifies physical death. It is seen as the gateway to heaven, to eternal rest and to the great celestial family reunion. Death is seen as a homecoming or graduation. It is in the after-life that we will finally see Jesus face to face and will instantly be made perfect.

The powerful and literal brainwashing of the doctrine of death can be seen in the Catholic Church's ritual of spreading ashes on the forehead of believers. This ritual – which has no New Testament foundation – dramatically illustrates the point that while the religious system may portray itself as pro-life in its advocacy of the rights of the unborn or in its stand against euthanasia or capital punishment, the "life" that the system seeks to protect and preserve is fundamentally different from the meaning Christ attaches to the term.

When Jesus spoke of eternal life, He was referring to the Life that is contained only in Him. Through Him, the believer enters into the life of the Melchisedec priesthood where we have no carnal genealogy, no beginning nor end of days. In His eyes, those who do not have this life are no better than dead men. ("Let the dead bury the dead" He said to a follower who hesitated following Jesus because he felt the need to bury his recently deceased father.) It is only through the intimacy of our relationship with Christ that we enter into Life and as this life takes hold of every aspect of our being, death in all its aspects is overcome. It is the second birth, which removes us from the realm of the Adamic life to the life of Christ, that is precious in the sight of God because it is only through the manifestation of the born again sons of God that the creation, in its entirety, will be delivered from the bondage of death.

While the religious system champions the rights pertaining to the Adamic life, it fights tooth and nail to prevent the second birth from occurring in the lives of Christians. This is symbolized in the 12th chapter of the book of Revelation by the dragon seeking to devour the manchild:

> ...and the dragon stood before the woman which was ready to be delivered, for to devour her child as soon as it was born. Rev 12:4

It is a reflection of the hypocrisy of religion that it opposes the manifestation in the physical of the crime, abortion, that it practices in the realm of the spirit. In fact, there is no evil, no perversion, no violence in the world, including death, that does not stem from the spiritual rebellion of the religious system against God.

Christianity's alliance with death, which borders on a form of spiritual necrophilia or death worship, is nothing new. According to the Word of God, the religious system that the Hebrew people were entangled in made what God calls in the book of Isaiah a "covenant with death". He goes on to say:

> And your covenant with death shall be disannulled and your agreement with hell shall not stand...
> Isa 28:18

In Hosea He says:

> I will ransom them from the power of the grave; I will redeem them from death: O death I will be thy plagues; O grave I will be thy destruction....
> Hos 13:14

These are just two examples of the wealth of scripture in the Old Testament, both in the books of the Law and the books of the Prophets, which reflect the fact that, especially with regard to His people, God views physical death ("the grave") as part of the curse and as something unclean and abhorrent. God's promise is that through the atoning work of Jesus, all aspects of the curse, including death, will be overcome. In the meantime, for the obedient and righteous in the Old Testament, the reward was a long and prosperous life. Nowhere in the Old Testament is death portrayed as the gateway to blessing as Christian theology views it.

The Unfolding Kingdom

The positive image of death as the time or place where we come into our inheritance – whether it be mansions, crowns of life, reunion with loved ones, the settling of scores, questions answered, rewards distributed to the worthy and punishment doled out to the disobedient or reprobate – perverts the very concept of inheritance. It is the *testator's* death and not the heir's death that makes inheritance possible. This distortion derives from a misunderstanding of the spiritual revelation Jesus was imparting when He expounded on the kingdom of God or the kingdom of heaven.

The fundamental problem is that the underpinning of virtually all Christian theology is the carnal understanding of heaven as a physical place inaccessible to us until a specific time (physical death). The fact is that not once in all four gospel accounts does Jesus equate or associate the kingdom of God or the kingdom of heaven with an afterlife.

What Jesus does do is describe the availability of a place in God in which He establishes total dominion over every aspect of the believer's life. This is a realm in the spirit that has nothing to do with time or space ("The time is coming and now is...") but it has everything to do with our readiness and willingness to sell all our "wealth" (which means, above all, renouncing our carnal understanding), to become as children, to die to everything in our life that is unlike Him, and to bear His reproach. This means taking Jesus at His word when He says: "He that believes in me shall never taste of death" and bearing the consequences of that faith – which are considerable.

There is a two-fold aspect to the revelation of the kingdom. In one respect, the fullness of God, including immortality, has always been available, by faith, to those who pleased God such as Enoch and Elijah; but in another respect there is a process across time of the unfolding of the revelation of Christ (or the "coming" of Christ), the culmination of which we see described in the book of

Revelation. In the Spirit, John sees the future of the Church as the mysteries of the Word are unveiled and as the doctrine of death is overcome. It is a "future" that is always available on an individual basis but will not come into total manifestation until the entirety of the Church is brought into the fullness of the revelation of Christ.

This ongoing process of revelation and the expanding availability to the Church of the fullness of God explains why Paul himself admits not to have attained to all that is available in God and seems reconciled to a physical death ("Whether we live or die, we are the Lord's"). Defenders of the religious system who point to Paul's death to justify their doctrine ("Even Paul died...") should keep in mind that Paul died a martyr's death – not as Christians today die, ravaged by old age or disease or victims of fatal accidents.

Nullification of the Atonement

In Paul's day, the Church was not ready to be unveiled as the fullness of God's glory – or God's third heaven – because revelation truth was as yet "unlawful" to be uttered or preached. After the martyrdom of Paul and the other apostles, the religious system stepped into the breach between the "God that is" (the historical Jesus or the second heaven) and the "God that is to come" (the fullness of the revelation of Christ in the Church or the third heaven). The system then created a theology forged in the imagery of the Adamic carnal mind. Faith based on the spiritual depth and subtlety of the Word was abandoned as scripture was given a literal and physical interpretation in which the doctrine of death – in effect, the antichrist – was enthroned.

The purpose of the doctrine of death – then as it is now – is to actively prevent the last enemy from being conquered by embracing that enemy and viewing it as a "friend". The more sophisticated theologies will concede that much of the fullness of God is available to believers in this life, but the religious system will never let Christians believe that physical death can be overcome because that would mean that sin can be conquered in our lives. As dispensers of forgiveness and grace on the one hand and guilt and condemnation on the other, the clergy of the system will do everything in its power to prevent Christians from entering into the fullness of the atonement.

The doctrine of death goes hand in hand with the teaching, common to every Christian denomination, that Christians remain sinners after experiencing salvation, the new birth and cleansing in the blood of Jesus. In subtle ways, the Law and along with it, judgment, condemnation and death, were re-introduced into Christian theology and, as a result, our understanding of the atonement was distorted.

As revelation and faith were replaced by morality and law, the atoning work of Jesus was made ineffectual and, indeed, unnecessary and His blood, through the unbelief engendered by the religious teachings of man, was rendered no more potent than the communal grape juice. How does a system that is founded on a teaching of imperfection answer this question: If the blood of Jesus and the Spirit of God that dwelt in Him, as it does in us, do not have the power to bring us into perfection, why would he require us to be perfect?

> Be ye therefore perfect, even as your Father in heaven is perfect. Matt 5:48

The system's response to this scripture is to add qualifiers which, in effect, nullify the power of the Word and the atonement. It is no coincidence that all the teachings of Paul and John that point to perfection or total deliverance from sin are either ignored or explained away. The goal of the religious system is to prevent the formation of that Bride that is without spot or wrinkle which is the culmination of God's plan for the creation.

Hidden Manna

The ultimate purpose and will of God is to experience Himself in flesh form – not just in the body of an individual Son as He manifested himself in Jesus – but in a multi-membered body, a body not limited by the dimensions of time and space as Jesus was. In Jesus, the Father could only be incarnated in one place at a time. In the Church, His incarnation can be a million-fold. The means to accomplish this divine purpose is through the mystery of the Word. Although Jesus conquered death, hell and the grave for all men, we enter into our inheritance only through the preaching of revelation truth that takes God's people beyond the common-sense, carnal understanding of the Word.

The Word starts to become flesh in us and we are born again as we receive the revelation of the kingdom in our spirit man and we begin to "see" the kingdom of God. The birth of the spirit man must be nourished by the milk of the Word, which provides the groundwork from which God builds His edifice in us. Even at the milk stage, the mind of man must be anointed by the Spirit of God in order to grasp the meaning of the Word.

To understand the Word as God intended it to be understood, the believer must be filled with the same

Holy Ghost that inspired those who wrote the Word. Only the Spirit of God in us can search the deep things of God. This milk stage is typified by the Holy Place in the temple where the priests ministered in the presence of the golden candlestick, the showbread and the altar of incense. Each item symbolized the Church in its aspects as the Light of the world, bread for the hungry and intercessors before the throne of God.

To enter the realm beyond the veil, the believer must move from the milk of the Word to the meat of the Word, which is typified by the manna that was hidden in the Ark of the Covenant contained in the Holy of Holies. This is the part of the temple that was not illuminated by either natural light (the human understanding of the carnal mind) or candlelight (the light of the Church) and from which all were excluded except the High Priest (sons of God). Once Christians become aware of the availability of this realm, the factors that hold them back are precisely those aspects that are typified by the darkness and exclusivity of the physical Holy of Holies.

The process of acquiring this hidden manna and unlearning the doctrine of death will relegate the believer to a place – socially, emotionally, spiritually and psychologically – of isolation, not only from the rest of the Body of Christ, but also from the human frame of reference. It is a spiritual no-man's-land or wilderness where God tries the faith and courage of His sons. It is the place outside the camp where we go forth unto Him bearing His reproach. But for all those who travel this path that no fowl knoweth, rest assured that it will be said of them:

> Who is this that cometh out of the wilderness like pillars of smoke, perfumed with myrrh and

frankincense, with all powders of the merchant....Who is this that cometh up from the wilderness leaning on her beloved?
Song of Solomon 3:6 & 8:5

The Mystery of Our Union In God

We know that the composer of the Battle Hymn of the Republic was truly a son of God because he was inspired to write these words: "In the beauty of the lilies Christ was born across the Sea: With a Glory in His bosom that transfigures you and me..." The Father showed me that it is in the bosom that the mysterious union transpires between the Father and the Son, Jesus and the sons of God and the Bride and the Bridegroom.

Why the bosom? Because it is where the heart is located and where the child is nurtured and fed. In addition, it is the bosom that spiritually represents the place where the throne of God is housed within us, surrounded by the 24 elders represented by our rib cage. As we trace the word throughout Scripture, we can see the various facets of this union of the bosom.

The union begins in the bosom of the Father who was revealed to Abraham by the name El Shaddai, or the Breasted One. The gospel of John 1:18 tells us:

No man has seen God at any time: the only begotten Son, which is in the bosom of the Father, he has declared Him.

Notice that John uses the present tense. Everything that Jesus was during His historical ministry and everything that He is eternally derives from the fact that He resides in the bosom of the Father. He continually felt His heartbeat, was fed by Him, knew His thoughts. And just as the Son is in the bosom of the Father, Isaiah 40:11 declares that we are in the bosom of the Son:

> He shall feed his flock like a shepherd: he shall gather the lambs with his arm, and carry them in his bosom, and shall gently lead those that are with young.

We see this portrayed in the last Passover when the beloved disciple, John, leaned his head on Jesus' bosom. But the mystery also encompasses the union within the Body of Christ. Because the Word declares that all who are joined to Christ are one spirit, we carry in our bosom all the saints and the cloud of witnesses. Oh Glory! We can see this pointed out beautifully in Numbers 11:12 as a frustrated Moses complains to God:

> Have I conceived all this people? Have I begotten them, that thou shouldest say unto me, Carry them in thy bosom as a nursing father beareth the sucking child, unto the land which thou swarest unto their fathers.

The most glorious aspect of this union is the reality that we carry the fullness of the Godhead, as our

Bridegroom, in our bosom. This is seen in the symbolism of the Song of Solomon 1:13 as the Bride speaks of the mystery of her union with the Beloved:

> A bundle of myrrh is my well beloved unto me. He shall lie all night betwixt my breasts.

What is the night season referred to here? It is the time before the full unveiling and manifestation of God's sons. It is the time that God has set aside for the preparation and perfecting of His army. It is the time that the Glory we now contain within us is shrouded by our earthen vessels just like the torches carried by Gideon's army. This night season is what Peter was describing in Acts 3:20-21:

> And he shall send Jesus Christ, which before was preached unto you: Whom the heaven must receive until the restitution of all things, which God has spoken by the mouth of all his prophets since the world began.

The heaven that receives Christ until the appointed times of restitution is contained in the bosom of the Bride where He lies waiting to be revealed to the creation as the bright and morning star. We can see a description of the Glory that is contained in our bosom – a glory that will transfigure the entire creation – in Revelation 11:19:

> And the temple of God was opened in heaven, and there was seen in his temple the ark of his testament: and there were lightnings, and voices, and thunderings, and an earthquake, and great hail.

Because of the mystery of our union with God, we **are** that temple in heaven that is opened to reveal the fullness of the Father. The creation is groaning for the manifestation of the Glory of God to be revealed in His sons. The creation is waiting to be able to say: "Mine eyes have seen the Glory of the coming of the Lord...."

Language

What are words worth
But of His perfect Love to tell
(deeper than the thoughts of man);
A quarry of diamonds crystallizing divinity:

Love
Love Love
Love Love Love
Love Love
Love

Word of God, flaming Lexicon, blaze across these synapses
To make me one with You.

Made in the USA
Las Vegas, NV
16 March 2022

45765709R00083